Virgil L. P. Blake
Editor

Mapping Curricular Reform in Library/Information Studies Education: The American Mosaic

Pre-publication
REVIEWS,
COMMENTARIES,
EVALUATIONS . . .

"**T**he title, *Mapping Curricular Reform in Library/Information Studies Education: The American Mosaic,* better conveys the importance of this book for the education of library and information professionals in the 21st century. It stands among the rare attempts to deal with curriculum revision in a world of shifting demographic ballasts. In the next century, data show that the United States will become a nation with no minorities. Yet few educational programs have taken a hard look at how shifts in population should affect what they teach. This compilation of papers, edited by Virgil Blake, gives us some insight from which to start.

Among the pieces readers shouldn't bypass are two by Joseph Fernandez and Leslie Agard-Jones, both associated with the New York City Public Schools. They reflect on multicultural education,

its meaning as well as its process. Both affirm that multicultural education is not adequately housed in a separate course. Rather it is central to all learning, since all students need to know, understand, and respect their own cultures as well as those of others.

In his focus on multiculturalism and technology in the academic library Mario Charles, Baruch College Library, makes us face how little we have prepared librarians to use the evolving technologies to make the library a more receptive place for diverse populations. Karen Thorburn, Director of the Plainfield (NJ) Public Library, gets to the heart of why students of diverse backgrounds fail to opt for careers in librarianship. Lack of awareness of the work we perform and its impact on quality of life must be addressed, if we are to change the limited progress library education has made in recruiting and retaining people of color.

While several of the papers are written by librarians for librarians, William Welburn, of the University of Iowa, speaks directly to library educators. In "Moving Beyond Cliche," he describes librarianship as a mediating profession in the dynamic interplay between people and information.

In a society questioning the need for affirmative action, making multicultural education a centerpiece for those entering our profession is even more crucial. The argument that it moves our society further along in its quest for social justice is enough reason for me to urge librarians and library educators to pursue this book and pay attention to its recommendations."

Betty J. Turock
Professor, Library and Information Studies, Rutgers University and President, American Library Association

"**A**long with recent works on approaches to multicultural librarianship, such as *Racial and Ethnic Diversity in Academic Libraries* edited by Deborah A. Curry et al. (The Haworth Press, Inc., 1994), *Multiculturalism in Libraries* edited by Rosemary R. Dumont et al. (Greenwood, 1994) and *Multiculturalism in the College Curriculum* by Marilyn Lutzker (Greenwood, 1995), *Mapping Curricular Reform* is a significant addition to the growing literature on multicultural reform in libraries and library school education. It provides us with a useful road map to the application of the elements of cultural diversity, to the content of library education, and even more important, with directions we must take in library information centers that service schools, the community, and academe. Why is this road map so useful? It provides us with the basic approaches to dealing with the new demography in America; the focus on ethnicity inside and outside our library institutions. Questions are raised about multicultural collection building in relation to the new multiethnic clientele in our communities and the need to recruit a faculty and professional staff that demonstrates sensitivity to cultural diversity in our society. It is noteworthy that intelligent and creative discussion is provided for us to deal with these challenging developments of a multiethnic society to the profession of librarianship.

The curriculum as a whole should reflect and deal with multicultural literature, efforts must be made to recruit a more diverse student body by studying the techniques followed in successful library schools. Several academic librarians are keen about insuring that curriculum changes, because of cultural diversity in academe, are supported by appropriate library resources. Further, there are recommendations for a more active and assertive role by librarians in seeking out opportunities to work with the faculty on culturally diverse materials. Again, we have a reminder that there is more need for sensitivity to ethnic differences in the reference interview.

It is clear that this volume contains many fruitful approaches in dealing with the impact of multiculturalism on libraries at all levels in preparation for the year 2000."

David Cohen, MSLS
Adjunct Professor of Library Science, Queens College of CUNY and Editor, EMIE Bulletin (EMIERT/ALA)

"**A**fter reading *Mapping Curricular Reform in Library/Information Studies Education* one can not question the near emergency need for multiculturalism to be incorporated into library/information science education. This monograph is a collection of selected papers that were presented at one of four regional conferences on multiculturalism and its implication for library/information science education.

Among the most exciting and surely one of the most valuable qualities of this work, is the fact that the contributions come from a diversity of library/information science and education professionals–administrators to the individuals working the front lines. Multiculturalism's relationship to library/information science is explored from nearly every facet of the field. The heterogeneity of contributors allows the authors to address multiculturalism as a whole, while at the same time provide insight into ethnically diverse populations of long term residents and recent immigrants from African, Asian, Hispanic, and other populations.

As the conference considered the spectrum of information centers, observations and actual accounts of incorporating multiculturalism into academic libraries, special libraries, and a variety of other information environments are also presented. These discussions cover issues that deal with the increasingly complex approach to collection development, sensitivities to the reference interview, impact of technology, information access, community outreach and involvement, staff training and recruitment of staff from diverse ethnic and minority backgrounds.

Investigating the many facets of library and information center operations in the multiculturalism age bring us back to the core of the work, "library/information science education reform." Attempts to incorporate multiculturalism into library/information science operations do offer material that could certainly provide a stepping stone for library/information science education. This collection of papers make it evident that there is much work to be done in the field. It is not only a seriously needed work, but an eye-opening read for anyone in the library/information science field."

Jane Greenberg
Teaching Fellow, University of Pittsburgh, School of Library and Information Sciences

Mapping Curricular Reform in Library/Information Studies Education: The American Mosaic

Mapping Curricular Reform in Library/Information Studies Education: The American Mosaic

Virgil L. P. Blake, PhD
Editor

The Haworth Press, Inc.
New York • London

Mapping Curricular Reform in Library/Information Studies Education: The American Mosaic has also been published as *Public & Access Services Quarterly,* Volume 1, Number 3 1995.

The Haworth Press, Inc., 10 Alice Street, Binghamton, NY 13904-1580 USA

Library of Congress Cataloging-in-Publication Data

Mapping curricular reform in library/information studies education: the American mosaic / Virgil L.P. Blake, editor.
     p. cm.
    Includes bibliographical references.
    ISBN 1-56024-740-1
    1. Library education–United States. 2. Information science–Study and teaching (Higher)–United States. I. Blake, Virgil L.P.
    Z668.M347 1995
    020'.71'173–dc20   95-37925
                                                 CIP

INDEXING & ABSTRACTING

Contributions to this publication are selectively indexed or abstracted in print, electronic, online, or CD-ROM version(s) of the reference tools and information services listed below. This list is current as of the copyright date of this publication. See the end of this section for additional notes.

- *Human Resources Abstracts (HRA),* Sage Publications, Inc., 2455 Teller Road, Newbury Park, CA 91320

- *Index to Periodical Articles Related to Law,* University of Texas, 727 East 26th Street, Austin, TX 78705

- *Information Reports & Bibliographies,* Science Associates International, Inc., 465 West End Avenue, New York, NY 10024

- *Information Science Abstracts,* Plenum Publishing Company, 233 Spring Street, New York, NY 10013-1578

- *INTERNET ACCESS (& additional networks) Bulletin Board for Libraries ("BUBL"), coverage of information resources on INTERNET, JANET, and other networks.*
  - JANET X.29: UK.AC.BATH.BUBL or 00006012101300
  - TELNET: BUBL.BATH.AC.UK or 138.38.32.45 login 'bubl'
  - Gopher: BUBL.BATH.AC.UK (138.32.32.45). Port 7070
  - World Wide Web: http: / / www.bubl.bath.ac.uk./BUBL/ home.html
  - NISSWAIS: telnetniss.ac.uk (for the NISS gateway)
  The Andersonian Library, Curran Building, 101 St. James Road, Glasgow G4 ONS, Scotland

- *Journal of Academic Librarianship, The: Guide to Professional Literature,* The Belmont Group, 1700 East Elliot Road, #6-512, Tempe, AZ 85284

- *Konyvtari Figyelo-Library Review,* National Szechenyi Library, Centre for Library and Information Science, H-1827 Budapest, Hungary

- *Library & Information Science Abstracts (LISA),* Bowker-Saur Limited, Maypole House, Maypole Road, East Grinstead, West Sussex RH19 1HH, England

(continued)

- *Marketing Executive Report,* American Marketing Association, 250 South Wacker Drive, Chicago, IL 60606
- *Newsletter of Library and Information Services,* China Sci-Tech Book Review, Library of Academia Sinica, 8 Kexueyuan Nanlu, Zhongguancun, Beijing 100080, People's Republic of China
- *Public Affairs Information Bulletin (PAIS),* Public Affairs Information Service, Inc., 521 West 43rd Street, New York, NY 10036-4396
- *Referativnyi Zhurnal (Abstracts Journal of the Institute of Scientific Information of the Republic of Russia),* The Institute of Scientific Information, Baltijskaja ul., 14, Moscow A-219, Republic of Russia

SPECIAL BIBLIOGRAPHIC NOTES

*related to special journal issues (separates)
and indexing/abstracting*

☐ indexing/abstracting services in this list will also cover material in any "separate" that is co-published simultaneously with Haworth's special thematic journal issue or DocuSerial. Indexing/abstracting usually covers material at the article/chapter level.

☐ monographic co-editions are intended for either non-subscribers or libraries which intend to purchase a second copy for their circulating collections.

☐ monographic co-editions are reported to all jobbers/wholesalers/approval plans. The source journal is listed as the "series" to assist the prevention of duplicate purchasing in the same manner utilized for books-in-series.

☐ to facilitate user/access services all indexing/abstracting services are encouraged to utilize the co-indexing entry note indicated at the bottom of the first page of each article/chapter/contribution.

☐ this is intended to assist a library user of any reference tool (whether print, electronic, online, or CD-ROM) to locate the monographic version if the library has purchased this version but not a subscription to the source journal.

☐ individual articles/chapters in any Haworth publication are also available through the Haworth Document Delivery Services (HDDS).

Mapping Curricular Reform in Library/Information Studies Education: The American Mosaic

CONTENTS

ABOUT THE EDITOR

Virgil L. P. Blake, PhD, is Associate Professor at the Graduate School of Library and Information Studies, Queens College, City University of New York. He has published over twenty-five articles and book chapters in library science publications, covering a wide range of topics involved either directly with or pertaining to the area of public services. He is an active lecturer/speaker at various workshops and conferences.

The American Mosaic:
Mapping Curriculum Reform–
An Introduction and Overview

Virgil L. P. Blake

SUMMARY. The Graduate School of Library and Information Studies at Queens College, CUNY conducted a series of four conferences on the impact of America's increasingly diverse society on the curriculum of schools of library/information science. Each of the conferences had a library/information center type as its focus. Each addressed issues of administration, reference services, and collection management. The overall findings and some recommendations are included. *[Single or multiple copies of this article are available from The Haworth Document Delivery Service: 1-800-342-9678, 9:00 a.m. - 5:00 p.m. (EST).]*

KEYWORDS. Multiculturalism and library/information science education, multiculturalism in librarianship, research issues for curriculum reform

The Graduate School of Library and Information Studies (GSLIS) has long been concerned with the increasingly diverse nature of American society, and the implications of these changes for the education of librarians and other information professionals. The GSLIS has been

Dr. Virgil L. P. Blake is Associate Professor at the Graduate School of Library and Information Studies, Queens College, City University of New York.

[Haworth co-indexing entry note]: "The American Mosaic: Mapping Curriculum Reform–An Introduction and Overview." Blake, Virgil L. P. Co-published simultaneously in *Public & Access Services Quarterly* (The Haworth Press, Inc.) Vol. 1, No. 3, 1995, pp. 1-13; and: *Mapping Curricular Reform in Library/Information Studies Education: The American Mosaic* (ed: Virgil L. P. Blake) The Haworth Press, Inc., 1995, pp. 1-13. Single or multiple copies of this article are available from The Haworth Document Delivery Service [1-800-342-9678, 9:00 a.m. - 5:00 p.m. (EST)].

1

fortunate to have as an Adjunct Professor David Cohen, a nationally recognized leader on multiculturalism, on its faculty for many years. Largely through his efforts the GSLIS has been offering a course in library services and materials for ethnic and cultural minorities. To further expand this effort and demonstrate its importance to the school, the GSLIS faculty at its 1991 annual retreat committed itself to the planning and organizing of a national conference on multiculturalism and its implications for library/information science education. Such a gathering would bring together library/information center professionals and library/information science educators to consider the implications of these social changes for the clientele, operation, services, and collections of library/information centers. These discussions, it was hoped, would suggest a foundation for curriculum changes that would enable the GSLIS to improve the preparation of professionals who will serve in this dynamic new setting.

In May 1992 the GSLIS applied for and received through Queens College a small Ford Foundation Diversity Grant. Subsequently the proposal was submitted to the Council on Library Resources for additional funding. As this was approved it became possible to revise the original concept of a national conference to four regional events. Dr. Virgil L. P. Blake was named coordinator for the series of conferences.

The final plan called for separate conferences for each type of library/information center, i.e., school library media centers, public libraries, academic and special/corporate libraries/information centers. The concluding meeting would focus on library/information science education. The basic structure for each of the four meetings was a keynote speaker to introduce the concept of multiculturalism and outline the implications of cultural diversity, including the price of ignoring it. A series of workshops or panel sessions would follow in which more specific aspects of the topic would be explored.

The first of the four meetings, held on October 21, 1992, focused on school library media centers. The co-sponsor of this event was the School Library Unit of the New York City Board of Education.

Dr. Andrew Hacker, Professor of Political Science of Queens College, CUNY and the author of *Two Nations, Black and White, Separate, Hostile and Unequal,* served as keynote speaker. In his address, Dr. Hacker pointed out the great changes taking place in American society and the social consequences of the increasing consciousness of ethnic and cultural groups. Unlike some other authors, he contended that returning to Americanization and the melting pot concept was not possible and that diversity had become part of American life. A clear implication of this development for librarians was an increasingly complex approach to collection development in libraries, an increase in challenges to library materials, and difficulties in securing and allocating funds for library services and materials.

At this meeting several concurrent workshops followed the keynote address. "The Challenge of Selecting Latino Materials" conducted by Dr. Virgil L. P. Blake of the GSLIS, outlined the diversity within the Hispanic community itself, the difficulties of relying upon the traditional reviewing media, and identified some of the major selection aids. Dr. Renee Tjoumas of the GSLIS noted in her "Criteria for Selecting Native American Materials" that few public libraries had selection guidelines for these materials and that most selection tools for Native American materials were both unknown and unused by public librarians. Dr. Karen Smith of the GSLIS surveyed newer African American materials and sources for children and young adults. Steve Delveccio, New York Public Library, focused on ways that school library media specialists and public librarians could help each other in fostering and supporting multiculturalism. "Multicultural Education," presented by Library Power, addressed the implications of initiatives like the Rainbow curriculum for school library media centers.

Focusing on academic and special/corporate libraries/information centers, the second conference took place on April 16, 1993. Co-sponsors (with the GSLIS) of this meeting were the American Society for Information Science, New York Chapter; the Association of College and Research Libraries, New York Chapter; the Library Association of the City University of New York; and METRO, the New York Metropolitan Reference and Research Library Agency.

Mr. Howard Dodson, Chief, Schomberg Center for Research in Black Culture, New York Public Library was keynote speaker. In his remarks, he drew upon his studies of American history and suggested that the key to curriculum reform was going back to the basics and re-creating all that follows from that base. In the case of American history the base, he suggested, was the Declaration of Independence and its statement that all men are created equal. From that foundation history books, particularly those intended as basic texts at all levels, are now in the process of being recast to include all peoples and their contributions to American life. Library/information science, it follows, could do well to ask the same types of fundamental questions and then proceed to reexamine the curriculum and its constituent elements.

In the first of the three ensuing panel sessions, Bernice R. Jones-Trent, Director of Montclair (N.J.) State College's Harry A. Sprague Library, detailed the procedures in place at that institution to ensure that changes in the curriculum are supported by the acquisition of adequate library resources. Claudia Gollop, a former CUNY librarian and currently on the faculty of the University of Pittsburgh, reported on her survey of the availability of multicultural materials in CUNY libraries. Ina Brown, Manager of Information Services at AT&T's Bell Laboratories, pointed out that many corporations are at the threshold of understanding the implications of a culturally diverse work force. As a result, library/information professionals in the corporate sector have the advantage of, in effect, defining their roles within the organization.

Lead off speaker of the second panel, Danilo H. Figueredo, Director of the Bloomfield (N.J.) College Library, addressed the problems of developing a multicultural collection. In his review of the collection development process, he pointed out alternative sources for reviews of materials, publishers with a special interest in multicultural materials, and other means to overcome obstacles in attaining a truly diverse collection. In her presentation Marilyn Lutzger, Chief Librarian of the John Jay College of Criminal Justice, CUNY, urged librarians to take an assertive stance and actively seek out opportunities to work with faculty to introduce materials relative to cultural diversity into their courses. Joshua Waller, of the Fashion Institute of Technology library's reference staff, discussed the need for more sensitivity toward cultural and ethnic differences in the reference interview and the need for reference librarians to actively select diverse materials for the reference collection.

In the third session, Dr. Lourdes Collantes, SUNY College at Old Westbury, reported the results of her recent perception study of naming objects and identifying subjects of abstracts of books. Since there was little consensus among her fairly homogeneous group of subjects, Dr. Collantes speculated upon the implications of these findings on an increasingly diverse student body. Mario A. Charles, a Reference Librarian at Bernard M. Baruch College, CUNY, examined the information requests emanating from a culturally and ethnically diverse student body.

The third in the series of conferences, entitled "Are You Ready for 2000? Change, Diversity and the Public Library," was held on September 10, 1993. Co-sponsors included the CUNY Center for the Study of Women & Society; METRO, The New York Metropolitan Reference and Research Library Agency; the New York Public Library; Brooklyn Public Library; Queens Borough Public Library; and the Long Island Library Resources Council.

Dr. Joseph Fernandez, President of School Improvement Services Inc. and the Council for the Great City Schools, was the keynote speaker. Dr. Fernandez emphasized that the setting in which the implications of cultural diversity are being most directly addressed is the inner city and its public schools. In responding to this presentation Dr. Virgil L. P. Blake pointed out that the fates of the public schools and the public library had historically been intertwined and that both public institutions had many common interests in the promotion of cultural diversity.

Administrative issues, i.e., how the public library can better prepare its staff to serve a diverse clientele was the focus of the first of the three panel sessions of this meeting. Dr. Alex Boyd, Director of the Newark (N.J.) Public Library, discussed the role of the library administrator in that process. He contended that this responsibility holds two dimensions. There are internal aspects, such as creating and maintaining an organizational climate that promotes the transformation of the staff to accepting the concept of multiculturalism and applying it in their relations with one another. The external aspect includes meeting with the board of trustees and other governmental bodies to promote multiculturalism and obtaining the funding necessary to support the broader range of services and collections that the enhanced mission of the library requires.

Maureen Sullivan, Maureen Sullivan Associates, is a library consultant whose specialty is staff development. A primary focus of her work has been sensitivity training of library professionals to improve intra-staff relationships. In her presentation, Ms. Sullivan outlined her strategy in these sessions and outlined practical steps that could be undertaken in any library setting. These steps are a necessary pre-condition in a library that has set out to broaden its appeal by addressing the information needs of its community's cultural/ethnic minorities.

Karen Thorburn, Director of the Plainfield (N.J.) Public Library, concluded this session with her analysis of the problems of recruiting and retaining cultural/ethnic minorities for careers in library/information services.

The library's relationship with its clientele was the topic of the second panel. Leslie Agard-Jones, Director of the Office of Multicultural Education for the New York City Schools, addressed the meaning of multiculturalism in education and its implications for public service institutions. Joshua Cohen, Outreach Consultant for the Mid-Hudson (New York) Library System, outlined procedures that a library could follow to identify unique client groups and their information needs. The first step toward enlarging the library's role, contended Raul Huerta, Director of the Frank E. Gannet Library of Utica College, was to realize that the librarian and the public are "in this thing together." Only when that realization takes place will librarians begin to create programs and services to meet anticipated information needs rather than waiting for the public to come in and state their needs.

The final session of this meeting was devoted to collection development issues. Danilo Figueredo, Director of the George Talbott Hall Library at Bloomfield (N.J.) College, reviewed the problems of the collection development model as applied to developing a truly multicultural collection. Ingrid Betancourt, Newark (N.J.) Public Library, discussed one of the responses to this situation, the Multimac Project. This project is responsible for obtaining materials in a wide range of languages, publishes booklists of its acquisitions and serves as a resource for other public libraries in the state of New Jersey. A similar successful program, the New Americans Project of the Queens Borough Public Library, was then outlined by Elizabeth S. Hsu.

The concluding conference of the series was held on October 15, 1993. It was designed to consider the issues raised in the first three meetings and their implications for library/information science education. One change of format for this meeting was the use of two principle speakers at the keynote session. The first of these, Dr. W. David Penniman, President of the Council on Library Resources, outlined some revisions to library/information science education that might better prepare a wider range of professionals and reflected on the current rash of school closings. Following this address Kriza Jennings, Diversity Consultant for the Association of Research Libraries, reported on her work to date. Based upon a lengthy literature review and sixty site visits, Ms. Jennings offered a number of observations regarding multiculturalism in higher education and, more specifically, graduate education in library/information science. By and large faculty in library/information science do not yet perceive cultural diversity as a major concern. This is compounded by the location of many ALA accredited schools in areas far removed from major urban sites. This isolation from the most culturally diverse population centers in America only makes it easier to dismiss the phenomenon despite the fact that many of the graduates of these same programs will be employed in library/information centers serving increasingly diverse populations. Jennings also noted that many faculty have not worked in or with a library/information center for many years and have no concept of the changing nature of the user population.

Academic regulations and the lack of financial support for students, especially those from cultural and ethnic minorities, was another major concern. While the scarcity of fellowships/scholarships may not be totally within the domain of the schools to resolve; academic regulations are. Most schools, reported Jennings, are still structured for full time students. The unique needs of the part-time student must be recognized; many of them have child care responsibilities and need to work. This suggests that schools need to develop more flexibility in scheduling and time limits to obtain the degree.

On the positive side, Jennings found that schools of library/information science with more progressive programs from a multicultural perspective were those where the parent institution was itself committed to the concept. These schools also seemed to have a clearly stated set of goals and objectives to implement a program to attract and educate a diverse student body.

Jennings suggested that schools of library/information science should: (1) take steps to get faculty more directly involved with libraries/information centers serving diverse populations; (2) ensure that courses incorporate more examples and resources with a multicultural emphasis; (3) use various teaching styles encouraging some discussion and cooperative learning experiences; (4) recruit more faculty from cultural/ethnic minorities, especially in an adjunct role; (5) differentiate between international students and American born students from cultural/ethnic minorities; and (6) encourage the faculty to become more aware of the values they bring to the classroom and act accordingly.

Since the Association for Research Libraries, concluded Jennings, has completed this first phase of its diversity project, it will launch, in 1994, its Partnership Program with those institutions that are more aware of the implications of cultural diversity for libraries. The objective of this phase of the project will be to establish models for other library/information centers to emulate.

Following the featured speakers each member of the first panel outlined his/her personal/ethnic perceptions of cultural diversity and its implications for libraries/information centers. Rodney Lee, Director of the Roosevelt (N.Y.) Public Library, pointed out that the concept of multiculturalism had, finally, reached acceptance which, he felt, would lead to a better understanding of the background, traditions, heroes, and history of a number of cultural/ethnic minorities. There was a danger of this awareness leading to a sense of apartness. That would undermine the real objective of cultural diversity.

Dr. Peter Li, Department of Far Eastern Languages, Rutgers University, indicated that a major cultural difference between Asian American students and their peers was the Confucian tradition of memorization to pass exams. Given this background and tradition these students are very good at remembering facts and repeating them on demand. Being able to marshall facts to resolve a problem is alien to this tradition.

Michele Leonard, Executive Director of Spirit Guides, stated in her "Native Reflections" that Native Americans are unique in a number of ways. Unlike other cultural/ethnic minorities they are not growing in numbers nor are they concentrated in urban areas. Many of the problems facing Native Americans are far more basic than those faced by other minorities. Leonard concluded that a major effort will be required to place Native Americans on the same playing field as other minorities.

The complexity of serving the Hispanic community was outlined by Katharine M. Breen of the Queens Borough Public Library's New Americans Project. Since the Hispanic community varies so greatly in terms of its education levels, experience with libraries, and information needs, carefully detailed planning is required if the library expects to meet this audience's needs effectively.

Members of the second panel presented their professional perspective and their suggestions for change. Dr. William C. Welburn, University of Iowa, argued that one could not discuss multiculturalism without remembering its historical context. He noted the contrast between the ability of libraries/information centers to adapt automation and multiculturalism.

Dr. Hardy Franklin, Director of the Martin Luther King Memorial Library, Washington D.C., added that what was required was simply more emphasis on "customer relations." Librarians, especially public librarians, should make every effort to determine their clientele, both actual and potential, and their information needs. Once this was complete the library should follow through with focused programs designed to meet those needs. The logical place to instill these skills, Franklin argued, was the schools of library/information science.

Barbara Shinn, Coordinator of Media Services and secondary school librarian in the Brookline (Mass.) public schools, contended that revision of the curriculum in schools of library/information science, while helpful, might be only a partial response. Inserting more multicultural literature in courses, a practicum, and some joint courses on curriculum with schools of education were easy to suggest. More important than these, Shinn felt, were personal qualities that may be more properly considered recruitment issues. The best school library media specialists were those who genuinely liked children/young adults. They are not persons seeking a refuge from the classroom. A good school library media specialist must be flexible, a lifelong learner, and, most important, be willing to love each individual student and give them the understanding that librarians are there to help them succeed.

A major obstacle to effective recruiting of cultural/ethnic minorities to library/information service careers, in the view of Ana N. Arzu, Law Librarian, Office of the District Attorney, Borough of Queens, was the ignorance of what library/information professionals do. But, added Arzu, in its renewed concern to recruit minorities, library/information science education should not lower its standards.

Members of the third panel were asked to suggest guidelines for changes in the curriculum. Dr. Eleanor Armour-Thomas, of Queens College's School of Education, agreed that the place of multiculturalism in higher education has become a major concern in the United States. Responding to this concern has created a two part strategy. One facet of the current scene concerns intergroup relations, i.e., an effort to not only make all aware of the uniqueness of others but also improve the degree to which all interact. The second aspect is to do this while retaining excellence in the institution's academic programs. While there is some evidence that the nature of the student body is far different now, and there is some evidence that the social climate is very different, there is no real indication, added Armour-Thomas, that the numbers of students from cultural/ethnic minorities graduating has changed much. Retaining excellence while attracting more students from cultural/ethnic minorities carries with it added responsibilities for the university and its library. It means a redistribution of resources to be used by a now far more diverse student body. It follows that schools of library/information science will have to develop more refined approaches to the development of collections and the funding they will require. Developing these and other courses, added Dr. Getinet Belay of Rutgers University's Department of Communications, will require drawing more extensively from the research in allied fields including education, psychology, anthropology, and, most importantly, cross cultural communications.

Dr. Elfrieda Chatman, University of North Carolina-Chapel Hill, felt that some of the guidelines to curriculum revision could be found in her research on information use in non-traditional audiences. Her studies to date have indicated that there are four factors at work among the information poor. These include: (1) risk taking, i.e., should I reveal that I need to know this or am I better off by not sharing this; (2) secrecy, the refusal to share information if it is felt it will put one in a worse position; (3) deception, i.e., not wanting others to know something or not knowing but pretending to; and (4) situational relevance–if something is not viewed as relevant it will not be used or valued. In considering the redesign of the curriculum schools of library/information science should be aware of these factors as elements of cross cultural communication.

REFLECTIONS

The original impetus for this series of conferences was to determine the degree to which the curriculum of schools of library/information science may need revision to improve the preparation of new professionals who will serve a clientele which is going to be far more diverse than that now encountered by information professionals. In each of the first three conferences attendees were invited to complete evaluation forms which specifically asked the respondents' feelings about the curriculum and suggestions for change. In none of these meetings did the respondents suggest major revisions. The vast majority suggested adding multicultural elements to the existing curriculum. A few suggested a specific course in multicultural librarianship, something the GSLIS at Queens College has offered for over two decades.

On the surface it would appear that these librarians, despite the comments of many speakers on the difficulties facing part-time students in most programs, are basically satisfied with the curriculum. Adding more examples, sources, and time with literature devoted to multicultural themes would seem to be all that is required. The easy answer is to say that the answer to the question "What is required in curriculum reform?" is "Not much." But one should keep in mind that these are the survivors of the process. These respondents may well be those most nearly like us. To ensure that this facile answer has validity, I would suggest a survey of cultural/ ethnic minority students who were recruited into an M.L.S. program but who failed to complete that program. This failure analysis may reveal more about the curriculum and how it is perceived while simultaneously becoming a valuable tool for curriculum assessment. A study of selected ALA accredited schools would be sufficient to indicate whether additional work was required.

A second theme that emerged from each of these conferences was the issue of recruitment. Schools of library/information science had not done an effective job of ridding the profession of the stereotype (Arzu). Nor have they done a particularly effective job at aggressively recruiting students from cultural/ethnic minorities. Several of the speakers (Thorburn, Jennings, Arzu, Welburn, Shinn, and Brown) indicated that until more effective recruiting succeeds in attracting more minorities to the profession, we will have to use the stopgap approach of educating majority students in cross cultural communication.

To facilitate progress toward a student body more reflective of the public it will serve, a second study needs to be considered. This would involve the identification of those schools most successfully recruiting students from cultural/ethnic minorities and subsequently examining the reason(s) for their success. Surveying entering students to determine the factor(s) for their selection of a particular program should be the technique used. Past research suggests that a prime factor in this decision is personal recommendations from graduates. This suggests that schools successful in recruiting cultural/ethnic minority students in the past will continue to do so. If there are strategies to be emulated, this line of inquiry ought to be pursued.

A third issue that came to the fore in this series was the role of the faculty. Jennings' observations that faculty, by and large, do not perceive multiculturalism as a major concern seems valid. This is actually a good news, bad news situation. A study by Futas and Zipowitz indicates that a large proportion of the current faculty will retire by or shortly after 2000. One of the implications of this is that current junior faculty and those now completing doctoral programs will play a major role in the transformation of schools of library/information science. Working from ALISE statistics, Dr. Kathleen McCook of the University of South Florida, in a recent *Library Journal* article, was encouraged by the number of minority students now in doctoral programs. Such optimism is not shared here since these ALISE reports do not take into account the career plans of those doctoral students. This suggests a third study–a survey of current doctoral students, especially those from cultural/ethnic minorities, to ascertain the number of these students considering library/information science education as a career, at least on an adjunct basis. This would provide some baseline data on the feasibility of Jennings' suggestion to aggressively recruit minority faculty.

This project began with its focus on the curriculum. In the process of examining the curriculum's responsiveness to America's increasingly diverse society these conferences suggested that the curriculum can not be studied in isolation. It is intimately tied to problems of recruitment of new professionals and faculty development. All three require a major effort. In turn these efforts are directly related to the future of library/information science education. Concurrent with this, as Welburn pointed out, is the issue of continually evolving information technologies. As the two research areas work toward each other, the structure of the new approach envisioned by Penniman will be clarified.

These conferences are only a preliminary step on the human side of the research into the future of library/information education. They have indicated questions to be investigated rather than a resolution of the issue of curriculum reform. But that alone is important.

In this volume are many of the original presentations prepared for one of the conferences. Included is a bibliography of articles which served as the basis for many of the other presentations. Together the essence of the four conferences has been preserved.

The Status of Public Education in Our Nation's Large Urban Areas

Joseph Fernandez

SUMMARY. The vast majority of America's cultural/ethnic/linguistic minorities are found in the nation's 50 largest cities. The problems that will eventually be faced by all communities are being confronted in these large cities first. While there are many problems, there are also a number of encouraging trends. Suggestions for continued improvement are made. *[Single or multiple copies of this article are available from The Haworth Document Delivery Service: 1-800-342-9678, 9:00 a.m. - 5:00 p.m. (EST).]*

KEYWORDS. Urban schools, cities–social situation, minorities in the cities, multiculturalism

I have been asked to speak to you today about cultural diversity and its implications for public service institutions. I can not come at this topic of cultural diversity by any other direction than through public education and the cities. There is no American education–now or in the future–without its Great City Schools. Nowhere does the national resolve to strengthen our children's education face a tougher test than in our inner cities. Every problem is more pronounced there, every solution harder to implement. The litany is

Dr. Joseph Fernandez is President of both School Improvement Services, Inc. and the Council of the Great City Schools, Washington, DC.

[Haworth co-indexing entry note]: "The Status of Public Education in Our Nation's Large Urban Areas." Fernandez, Joseph. Co-published simultaneously in *Public & Access Services Quarterly* (The Haworth Press, Inc.) Vol. 1, No. 3, 1995, pp. 15-26; and: *Mapping Curricular Reform in Library/Information Studies Education: The American Mosaic* (ed: Virgil L. P. Blake) The Haworth Press, Inc., 1995, pp. 15-26. Single or multiple copies of this article are available from The Haworth Document Delivery Service [1-800-342-9678, 9:00 a.m. - 5:00 p.m. (EST)].

now familiar to you: poverty, drug abuse, family instability or no families at all, aging buildings and facilities, dropouts, teen pregnancy, poor health care, violence, racism and bigotry, AIDS, limited English language proficiency, and disabilities and malnutrition. And efforts to address these must be conducted in an atmosphere of enormous political, demographic, economic, cultural, social and religious complexity and diversity–usually with precious little dollars and backing.

It is often asked, however, why anyone should care. Why should the larger community want to help solve problems that are so daunting, so complex, remote, costly, entrenched and divisive. The reasons are actually uncomplicated.

First, it is in America's best self interest to care. Urban children take up too large a portion of America's total children to expect that the country can survive without them. And urban children, more than any others, provide the tint and hue of the American Mosaic. Of the nation's 15,000 school districts, our largest 50 city school systems educate 38% of the nation's limited-English proficient children, 25% of the nation's poor children, and 14% of its disabled children. About 40% of our nation's African-American, Latino, add Asian-American children are educated each day in our major city schools. In fact, our total enrollment–not population–would qualify us as the 80th largest of the 160 countries in the United Nations and certainly the most culturally diverse.

Consider this: if the graduation rate for urban schools equaled the national average, the Great City Schools would have graduated 295,521 students in 1990-1991 instead of 214,253. At the current 28% tax rate, the Federal tax on the additional lifetime earnings of those extra 81,268 individuals, had they graduated, is large enough annually to double the present Congressional appropriation for elementary and secondary education, increase Federal AIDS research five-fold, or boost Federal drug prevention efforts by a factor of ten–efforts that benefit the entire nation, not just the cities.

Second, unless action is taken to meet the challenges of urban education and its cultural diversity, our problems will soon enough become reality in all but the most elite of the nation's schools.

Finally, the country has a moral imperative, grounded in our own Constitution, to strive for individual justice and equality for its citizens. Education is the soundest way of endowing those rights and those of us who serve the public have a responsibility to respond to the changing community. The nation can not afford to play a game of containment with us, hoping that our problems will stay inside the city limits. It is already too late for that and besides, we are too large a portion of the country and its future for such a strategy to work. For our part, we can not continue to pretend that we can do this job alone. The problems we face in our schools are so immense and so entangled with the problems of our nation and its cities, that we cannot hope to meet them ourselves. Nor can the nation realistically hope to meet its own goals and stay economically competitive without us. It is how I come at the state of American education and what must be done to save it–through the cities.

Let me take a minute to describe where we are in urban education, draw your own conclusions about where American schools must be, given what I have just described, then allow me to talk about what I think should be done and what we are doing specifically. It is a good news–bad news story. Let me give it to you in equal measure, goal by goal.

First is preschool education and readiness for school. Despite the national consensus about the importance of early development, the statistics are frightening:

- Some 15-20% of all babies in the country are born exposed to illegal drugs;
- Some 7% of all babies, and 13% of African-American babies are born with low birth weight;
- Some 20% of all pre-kindergarten students are not vaccinated against polio;
- Only 33% of eligible children receive Head Start services; and
- Some 25% of pregnant women receive no prenatal care during the first trimester.

It is an area, however, where urban schools may be doing better than America's schools, in general, in developing solutions and an example of how this public institution is responding to a problem that is exacerbated by an influx of immigration. There are promising signs in our city schools:

- Some 58% of our urban school districts now assess the readiness of children for school using a combination of measures of cognitive development, immunizations, health, social development, weight and age.
- Some 53.1% of our first graders had a full day kindergarten in the same school where they are now in first grade.

The bad news, though, is that some 20% of our urban school districts still use only a birth certificate to assess readiness for school. We should do better than that. We should do better at placing health services, family support programs, and child care services directly in our schools. Few efforts would provide greater pay-off, than efforts by us to coordinate our social, family and health activities with those of other public and private agencies and groups throughout the cities. It is an area where urban schools are already doing better than most schools but where we could be models for the nation.

Second, is the area of dropouts where urban schools have considerable more difficulty. Here the statistics are also troubling but getting better:

- Only 69% of students entering high school in 1986 graduated in 1990.
- Pregnancy still leads the list of reasons why girls dropout, with over one million teen pregnancies each year.
- The dropout gap between African-American students and whites appears to be closing but remains wide with Hispanic students.

While our urban schools continue to have serious problems in this area, there are positive signs that suggest that we are doing something right.

- The median annual dropout rate in our urban schools dropped from 10.6% in 1988-1989 to 8.8% in 1990-1991.
- The median four year dropout rate in urban schools declined from 32.1% to 26.1% in 1990-1991.

The bad news is that our rates are still about twice as high as the national average. The dropout rates particularly of our Hispanic youngsters are not budging much. The rates for those youngsters are in the neighborhood of 10-15% annually.

One of the promising trends nationally, however, is that the drop-out rates among our African-American youngsters is declining to a level that is nearly comparable to white students. My guess is that this positive development nationally can be traced directly to urban schools and the efforts they have been making over the last ten years, and is a clear indication of the link between the cities and how the nation fares. One thing we have learned over the years is to tailor our programs better to the myriad reasons why youngsters drop out of school.

Third is achievement. The national figures here are also not good and are obviously now driving much of the current debate on standards and assessments:

- The United States ranks approximately 12th of 14 nations on international tests of mathematical and scientific knowledge among 13 year olds.
- Some 58% of 13 year old students in the United States display only moderate reading ability.
- Only 18% of 8th graders in the United States meet new national standards in mathematics.

There is evidence that our urban schools are making progress here too, although the bad news continues to outstrip the good.

- About 67% of urban school districts showed increasing achievement test scores in reading and mathematics between 1988-1989 and 1990-1991 at the elementary grade levels, and about half did in the second grades.
- The average urban student scored at about the 50th percentile in mathematics in 1990-1991, although lower in reading.
- Urban public school students were completing advanced placement or international baccalaureate courses in reading, mathematics and science at about twice the national average.

These are obviously promising indicators but there are discouraging ones too. Only one-third of our urban students have completed a first year course in algebra by the end of their 10th grade.

The achievement of our African-American and Hispanic students is far too low. Only 10% of our African-American students score in the top quartile in mathematics by the 10th grade, although a full 25% had in the 2nd grade. We enroll 32% of the nation's Hispanic youth, yet we produce fewer than 1,000 Hispanic students each year who score in the top quartile in mathematics. We should do better than this in urban America. The new standards development process may help in this regard but more headway can be made with more cooperative learning models, less tracking and remedial skills efforts, and more intensive instructional approaches.

Fourth is teaching and teachers. While we have some of the most dedicated and talented teachers in the world teaching in schools in the United States, there are danger signs:

- A substantial portion of the nation's teachers are expected to retire in the next ten years.
- Fewer African-Americans and Hispanics are pursuing careers in teaching.
- The nation's schools spend precious little of their resources on professional development and training for teachers.

Urban schools, by and large, reflect national trends in this area, although there are positive indicators as well, including:

- Some 98.6% of our urban secondary-grade English teachers are certified to teach in English and 96.9% of our secondary grade mathematics teachers are certified to teach mathematics.
- Urban teachers are more likely to be more experienced than the average teacher.

The bad news is that we are now not able to pay our teachers much more than the national average, thereby cutting our ability to attract individuals willing to work in our most difficult schools. In addition, the demographics of our teachers is almost the exact opposite of our students and the shortage of teachers in urban areas is about 2.5 times higher than the national average. Our ability to correct these trends will rest largely on our willingness to spend more on professional development, our ability to improve working conditions in our inner city schools, and our aggressiveness in reaching out to the African-American, Hispanic, and Asian-American communities to encourage more individuals from there to seek teaching in our schools as a career. Like the area of preschool education, it is an area in which urban schools can easily serve as national models.

Fifth is our post-secondary opportunities. Here we are paying the price now for years of under-investment in education and literacy, and shifting demographics:

- Some 27 million Americans are judged to be illiterate.
- The average youth unemployment rate is about 15-20%, although about 30% in the inner cities.
- About 75% of all new jobs between now and the year 2000, according to the U.S. Department of Labor, will be in the suburbs.

Urban schools are showing some positive signs in areas here over which they have some control but there are many aspects of what happens here that our schools have trouble affecting:

- Some 41.8% of our graduates entered or planned to enter four year colleges or universities, a rate higher than the national average.

But our good news here may be an artifact of high dropout rates. The numbers do show, however, that if you stay in school–even an urban public school–your chances of going to college are as good as anybody from anywhere.

Finally, are the challenges of safety, drug abuse and facilities. These are areas where schools nationally are facing serious problems but where the public has a difficult time investing resources to correct the problems. The national statistics are troubling:

- Each day there is estimated to be about 16,000 crimes on or near school property.
- Some 100,000 students bring weapons to school each day.
- Drug use among teens continues to be high despite promising trends recently.
- There is some $50 to $100 billion in capital needs across the nation for our school facilities.

These signs clearly indicate a serious problem, not just for urban schools but for the American society. I think we need to see squarely that these are not just problems of kids–these are adult problems. It is adults who manufacture and distribute the guns, who produce and show the violence on television, and who abuse and beat our children–kids don't do this, we as adults do.

What does all this add up to? What should we be doing to save our schools? My hunch is that we as a nation are doing better with our public school system than most people realize and what most critics suggest. But even if the critics are entirely wrong, and they're not, there is no reason to think that our schools shouldn't be substantially improved. Our economic global competitiveness certainly rests on it, as does our domestic tranquility. And here is where I am brought back to urban schools with all of their cultural diversity and their centrality to our national purpose and our desire to lead the world educationally. Let me start at home base with urban schools themselves and what they could be doing better. And I do want to be up front about our thinking that we can do better in lots of areas. I have talked about some already but let me suggest a few more. Some of them actually cost surprisingly little money.

Here is my "Top Ten List" for improving urban schools and improving the nation:

1. Urban schools not only need to be more open to educational reform, but actually lead it. There are many cases where they have, including the schools in New York City, Houston, San Diego, Dade County, Pittsburgh, Rochester, Milwaukee, Cleveland and others. In fact, much of the reform movement that has now been somewhat co-opted by the states grew out initiatives and experiments in city schools. Yet urban education is often viewed as entrenched, immovable, self-protective and sluggish with bureaucracy. *In too many instances this is the case,* but the reformers among us can easily serve as models to the rest. It is, in fact, good for us to reform and it is better yet to reform ourselves–urban schools are in the best position to do that. And make no mistake–the reform agenda celebrates our diversity and sees it as a strength and not a weakness.

2. Urban schools need to increase their collaborative arrangements with the community at large, and again by definition, this impacts our diverse communities. I said earlier that I believe that closer collaboration with other public and community agencies was necessary to deliver comprehensive services to our children. I will expand that here to include the churches, business community, the media, the suburbs, the Mayors and others. It also means keeping our facilities open to the community and designing our programs around the schedules and needs of the community, not our own. *As far as I am concerned, urban education cannot solve the problems faced by society alone.* That does not mean we shouldn't be involving ourselves in issues no one else will touch; it does not mean we are asking for help from all quarters now that we have accepted the challenge.

3. Urban schools need to stop treating parents as the enemy. Urban education has amazingly few friends. Not only can it not afford to alienate anyone, it must develop better strategies to reach out to parents on whatever terms or grounds they find themselves. We should not be treating them as our number one customer but also our number one ally. It is for that reason that I support legislation to add another national goal on parental involvement. We must understand the many different communities that we must interact with. *We must be inclusive and not exclusive.*

4. Urban school leaders need to stop chewing themselves up on political agendas. I am not sure how to do this but there are examples galore in every city where the fractured and desperate nature of the community is leading educational leadership into gridlock that would make Washington pale in comparison. Part of what is going on can be traced to the extreme poverty and needs of the urban community badly wanting a quality education and a future, but the desperation has begun to turn inward in the form of bureaucratic cannibalism.

5. Urban schools need to do everything they can to stop sorting and tracking students, and to raise the standards and expectations for their children. Too much of schooling, not just in cities but everywhere, is caught up in the unwitting sorting and

tracking of students by ability or perceived ability. Too often the results lead only to sorting by race, sex, and income and have nothing to do with the abilities or efforts of these students. *We must believe that all children can learn, and practice that belief.*

6. Urban school boards, administrators and teachers should think more positively of their work. People working in urban schools have listened so long to people bashing them and their work that I think they have started to believe and act on it. It has lead to a defensiveness about what we do and a corresponding reflex instinct when we are criticized. In fact most of the people I know in urban education are some of the most talented, dynamic and intelligent people working anywhere.

7. Urban schools need to down-size anything that touches children. In New York I started a process that has lead to a series of smaller high schools. I think it is important that we reduce the size of our urban schools, particularly the high schools, even if they are only schools-within-schools. Children need warmth and individual attention to thrive and it is hard to give it to them with schools the size of factories.

8. Urban schools need to help break down the artificial barriers between managers and teachers. Outside of students and parents, teachers should be our best friends in education but often they are not and we sometimes ensure it by how we act. Business has developed some very interesting models for how to establish more collaborative work settings and there is no reason why we should not be looking at testing those in our settings. Education is, after all, a human endeavor where the merits of all our people need to be respected.

9. Urban schools need to devote more time and effort to professional development, research and strategic planning. So much of our work in urban education is crisis oriented that we devote precious little time to planning for anything more than the next board meeting. Because education is a long-term endeavor, we need to plan and think long-term.

10. Urban schools need to increase, not shy away from, their commitment to and emphasis on multiculturalism. Urban

schools often take a lot of heat for their efforts to celebrate and enhance the diversity of their students and teachers. But urban schools, in fact, are well ahead of a nation that will need to do the same thing very shortly. The nation could take a lesson from us, here.

There are also things I think that the states and the Federal government could do to help us. Some of it has to do with money. While I don't think money cures all, I am a firm believer that money matters in schools like it does everywhere else. I saw it everyday in my work from the time I was a high school mathematics teacher in Miami through the time I served as Chancellor of the New York City Public Schools. Part of that belief rests on the fact that urban schools do not have the resources of other school systems. Our data indicate that the average large city school system spent about $5,200 per student in 1990-1991 while the average suburban school system spent $6,073. That disparity between urban schools and the suburbs amounts to nearly $22,000 more for a class of 25 whose needs are not as high as their peers in the suburbs. The long and short of it is that America is getting what it is paying for in urban education. I repeat: There is no future for America that fails to include its Great City Schools. *The disparity in funding between rich and poor schools is a national disgrace.*

To date the states have been slow to move to correct the situation without court intervention. Besides pressing to correct these inequities, I would urge the states and the governors to urge Congress to help on this front by enacting legislation that makes the Federal government an actor in education that reflects the national need. The governors should be pressing Congress for a major new education spending initiative or trust fund to help equalize the disparities and to deliver on the opportunity standards that many in the Congress are calling for as part of the Clinton administration's reform bill. Congress, for its part, should not complete the process of reauthorizing the Federal Elementary and Secondary Education Act without approving a sizable new initiative to help poor schools, particularly in urban and rural areas, to meet the national goals. This is the last reauthorization before the year 2000. Both Congress and the Clinton administration should want to leave a legacy that includes more than setting standards and reforming current programs.

America's schools have traditionally been at the heart of the communities they serve. As the fundamental institutions they are in our history and evolution, public schools have been one of the few places where the economically advantaged mingled with the economically disadvantaged, and where the newly arrived Jamaican meets the Russian Jew and where the Dominican student sits next to the Korean student. Where over and over again this picture is played out in our public institutions and where ideally political, religious and ethnic boundaries would not exist. As a nation, America has literally entrusted its future to its public schools. This investment is doubly important in its urban schools, for they form one of the crucibles of American democracy today. They truly represent the cultural diversity that has always strengthened this country. They are, in fact, one of the last frontiers of our democratic ideal. The nation can not afford to survey our urban landscape–with its difficult terrain–and conclude that conquering our troubles is a lost cause. The year 2000 looms large and near. We–as a nation–can not arrive there without its city children. The alternatives are too bleak to imagine. We must engage our young people. We must make them feel that school is about them. We must change our institutions to meet the needs of our children.

Common Threads:
Public Education, Public Libraries and Urban America

Virgil L. P. Blake

SUMMARY. The historic relationship between the rise of public education and public libraries is noted. The similarities of problems facing both the urban schools and urban public libraries are noted. Since many of the suggestions for improvement of the urban public schools are equally apt for public libraries, the Urban Libraries Council and Council of the Great City Schools are natural allies. *[Single or multiple copies of this article are available from The Haworth Document Delivery Service: 1-800-342-9678, 9:00 a.m. - 5:00 p.m. (EST).]*

KEYWORDS. Urban public libraries, urban education and leadership, multiculturalism in the development of public domains

Public libraries and public education have shared common interests and common problems for nearly 150 years. It is not entirely coincidental that the first publicly supported public libraries were founded at the time Barnard and Mann were convincing people that it was in their best interests to create public schools. Nor is it

---

Dr. Virgil L. P. Blake is Associate Professor at the Graduate School of Library and Information Studies, Queens College, City University of New York.

[Haworth co-indexing entry note]: "Common Threads: Public Education, Public Libraries and Urban America." Blake, Virgil L. P. Co-published simultaneously in *Public & Access Services Quarterly* (The Haworth Press, Inc.) Vol. 1, No. 3, 1995, pp. 27-29; and: *Mapping Curricular Reform in Library/Information Studies Education: The American Mosaic* (ed: Virgil L. P. Blake) The Haworth Press, Inc., 1995, pp. 27-29. Single or multiple copies of this article are available from The Haworth Document Delivery Service [1-800-342-9678, 9:00 a.m. - 5:00 p.m. (EST)].

coincidental that the social and *proprietary* libraries were replaced by public libraries in the post-Civil War era when publicly supported elementary schools became part of the American landscape. Public libraries have always regarded themselves as an informal educational institution. The public library was soon labeled "the people's university." Some public librarians took their educational role very seriously and had grave reservations about the addition of fiction to a library's collection. Public libraries have had an enduring tie to public education and we are still intertwined. What is happening in public education and its fate is of great interest to librarians, especially public librarians and school library media specialists, because these public institutions deal with the same clientele and are supported by the same tax base. Consequently the issues facing public education are also facing public libraries. As Dr. Fernandez pointed out these problems will not remain isolated in urban America. In the small town in central New Jersey in which I live, the summer of 1993 saw several bias related incidents. It would appear that the issues raised by Dr. Fernandez are going to be recurring in the suburbs–some sooner than others.

As I listened to your talk I became aware of several close analogies that otherwise might never have occurred to me. Running through your survey of the urban scene one recurring theme was the greater degree of difficulties being faced by the Hispanic community. At Queens College's Graduate School of Library and Information Studies (GSLIS) African-American and Asian Americans are well represented in the student body. Hispanics are chronically under-represented. This is the group that the GSLIS has the most difficult time recruiting. Very few Hispanics apply to the GSLIS. Part of the reason for this is now perfectly clear. But this is an area in which both the schools and libraries have a common interest and goal. We both need to develop effective means of attracting talented Hispanics to serve as role models for others.

Another interesting area of common concern is the need to replace retiring professionals–those with the most experience. This is especially true in library/information science education where a study by Futas and Zipowitz[1] estimate that 30-40% of the current faculty could retire by 2000. Where are those new educators going to come from? Once again both institutions are facing similar problems. If people can not be recruited to the profession in the first place, where will the future faculty be recruited from?

In suggesting the necd to reach out and find allies, both public education and public libraries should take heed. Urban public schools and urban public libraries are natural allies. Combining much could be done.

As Dr. Fernandez has suggested there is no future for America without a future for the cities. I am convinced that whatever is going to happen to the cities is probably going to happen to New York City first. Many of the things that are so contentious to deal with now will provide an opportunity for a leadership role not just for other cities but also the suburbs who may not realize it yet but their time is coming.

REFERENCE

1. Elizabeth Futas and Fay Zipowitz, "The Faculty Vanishes; Accelerating Recruitments and Difficulty in Attracting New Educators Could Spell Disaster for the Profession as a Whole," *Library Journal,* 116 (September 1, 1991), p. 148-152.

Are You Ready for 2000?
Issues Raised by an Education
That Is Multicultural

Leslie Agard-Jones

SUMMARY. Multicultural education is defined. A true multicultural education rejects separation in favor of inclusivity and respect for differences. *[Single or multiple copies of this article are available from The Haworth Document Delivery Service: 1-800-342-9678, 9:00 a.m. - 5:00 p.m. (EST).]*

KEYWORDS. Multicultural education, multicultural curriculum

When I assumed the position of Director of the Office of Multi-cultural Education for the New York City Public Schools, in January, 1993 the Chancellor was Dr. Joseph A. Fernandez; the Deputy Chancellor for Instruction, to whom I reported, was Argie K. Johnson, the current Superintendent of Schools in Chicago; and the Chair of the central Board of Education was H. Carl McCall, currently the Comptroller of the State of New York. The public school system was in the middle of a process of reform with many policy changes being debated and initiated.

Leslie Agard-Jones is Director of the Office of Multicultural Education, New York City Public Schools.

[Haworth co-indexing entry note]: "Are You Ready for 2000? Issues Raised by an Education That Is Multicultural." Agard-Jones, Leslie. Co-published simultaneously in *Public & Access Services Quarterly* (The Haworth Press, Inc.) Vol. 1, No. 3, 1995, pp. 31-36; and: *Mapping Curricular Reform in Library/Information Studies Education: The American Mosaic* (ed: Virgil L. P. Blake) The Haworth Press, Inc., 1995, pp. 31-36. Single or multiple copies of this article are available from The Haworth Document Delivery Service [1-800-342-9678, 9:00 a.m. - 5:00 p.m. (EST)].

At that time, any mention of multicultural education brought recrimination and the charge that the Board, or more specifically, the Chancellor, was attempting to legitimize homosexuality and somehow participate in the recruitment of children to this lifestyle. Multicultural education was linked with the public school's condom distribution initiative, the HIV-Aids policy and the general view that the focus on social issues was deterimental to the learning process and an infringement on parental rights.

Multicultural education was then and still is the subject of a tremendous amount of distortion, misinformation and misunderstanding. It is my hope that you, each of you, in your particular roles will contribute to the effort to clarify and better understand what is meant by an education that is multicultural. What then, in my view, is an education that is multicultural? And what are some of the issues raised by such an education?

James Banks has defined multicultural education as "at least three things: an idea or concept, an educational reform movement, and a process."[1] Banks has been a major philosophical contributor to making an education multicultural in New York City, the nation and the world.

Primarily we must understand that an education that is multicultural involves content as well as process. A process in which our schools are transformed from being monocultural institutional representatives of our society, with all the inherent biases associated with monoculturalism, to one that is inclusive of our global village. The total school and its environment, not just the curriculum must be addressed.

Sonia Nieto defines an education that is multicultural as:

> . . . a process of comprehensive school reform and basic education for all students. It challenges and rejects racism and other forms of discrimination in schools and society and accepts and affirms the pluralism (ethnic, racial, linguistic, religious, economic and gender, among others) that students, their communities, and teachers represent. Multicultural education permeates the curriculum and instructional strategies used in schools, as well as the interactions among teachers, students and parents,

and the very way that schools conceptualize the nature of teaching and learning. Because it uses critical pedagogy as its underlying philosophy and focuses on knowledge, reflection and action (praxis) as the base for social change, multicultural education furthers the democratic principles of justice.[2]

In general, Nieto views multicultural education as antiracist and antidiscriminatory; as basic education; as being important for all students; as pervasive; as education for social justice; as a process; and finally, as a critical pedagogy.

The New York City Public Schools has defined multicultural education as:

> . . . an instructional approach designed to restructure the total school environment for the purpose of maximizing student achievement. It treats the cultural diversity of our students as a valuable educational resource. Its focus includes an understanding and appreciation of ethnic differences, and extends to areas of language, gender, race, socioeconomic class, religion, sexual orientation, age and to people with disabilities. It seeks to provide students with the knowledge, skills and attitudes required to become fully participating citizens in society, to promote harmonious relationships, and to encourage students to take positive action to effect needed change.

For some emphasis in definition must be placed on the historical inequities that plague our society. The past as prologue to the present and future. Concentration on the past, perceived as curricular issues, at times diverts attention from addressing the total environment. We must always be conscious not to limit multicultural education's applicability simply to curriculum.

These basic definitions are inclusive. Inclusivity, however, is one of those contentious issues around which controversy has sprung. The basic question of including sexual orientation, age, gender, people with disabilities–cross-cultural components–in any definition of multicultural education has been received with mixed reviews. Some would include gender but not age, or people with disabilities, and definitely not sexual orientation. Some would exclude all cross-cultural components. Others argue that the emphasis should be placed in one particular area or with one particular ethnic or racial group.

One of the cautions offered in multicultural education is the caution of over generalizing. However, given the number of ethnic groups found in each racial category, one often finds some generalizing. If I may illustrate, not all people of African descent are from the same ethnic group and/or class. There is a question of the extent to which African-American is inclusive of the Caribbean American or the person directly from the African continent. How does national identity, be it Jamaican, Haitian or Ghanaian, relate to the issues of race and ethnicity in identifying someone as an African-American? What role does class and gender or any other crosscultural component play within a particular ethnic or racial group?

The basic purpose of an inclusive definition is to respect that which is in each of us and makes us human. Our commonality, to some is not emphasized as much as our differences. We may do things differently, look differently, speak differently but are all part of one family. Respect for difference, respect for diversity is, and should be, an asset in our global village. We cannot continue to view difference, that we do not know or understand, as a deficit.

Another issue often raised is the idea that multicultural education promotes the separation of ethnic and racial groups and, in essence, disunites our community. Often it is described as particularistic multiculturalism. One in which the emphasis is on one particular group to the exclusion of others. Ignoring differences, ignoring the historical interethnic conflict while attempting to forge unity on the basis of commonalities often has tragic consequences. Our experience today in many parts of the world bears tragic testimony to this fact.

The fundamental base of multiculturalism is knowing oneself. From knowing oneself one moves to knowing others. The process of knowing others begins to open us up to a multicultural environment. Materials have to be made available to allow self and others to access knowledge that has not always been available on the diversity that makes up the human experience.

Language and its use is very important to an education that is multicultural. Use of some words in a particular context can reflect ancient or age old biases that we must confront. For example, when we speak of the West, how often do we consider West of what. Our frame of reference is primarily one that uses a perspective or view from Europe as the norm or basis for any observation. Insensitive use of language is not limited to calling someone by some racial or ethnic epithet. Additionally, as we address language, there are those who promote one language at a time when all of us should be increasing our efforts to become bi- and multi-lingual. Being multilingual is regarded as an asset in most parts of the world but in the United States, in some quarters, it is treated as a deficit. It is the diversity that is America, some would argue, that makes this country strong. Others seek, out of this diversity, one American culture in which, unfortunately, a particular group dominates and sets the standards for all other groups.

If we are really conscious of language, we would realize that in speaking of America as limited to the United States, we have eliminated the other inhabitants of North and South America. For those of us who live in the United States, we are exclusively America just as surely as the World Series, limited to teams in the United States and Canada, represents the whole world.

Associated with the idea of someone being afraid of the other is an example from a *New York Times* article on September 8, 1993, in which, a young man who happened to be Latino attempted to assist a car stuck on the railroad tracks whose occupants were Asian. They, fearing him, locked their doors and he was only able to get three of the occupants out of the car before it was struck by a train killing the person who remained in the car. Fear of the other, believing that some harm would result from this man cost that person her life.

All too often multicultural education has been equated simply with foods, festivals, and fashions–all components of multicultural education–but primarily superficial components. We must go beyond this superficial stage to develop a deeper understanding of the multicultural education process.

Multicultural education is not a separate subject, but an integral part of the educational process. Multicultural education is not separate from the 3R's, it is the 3R's. Schools will still have "See Spot run," but Spot will do so from multiple cultural perspectives. As librarians, seeking out and making such materials available will be one of your tasks.

An education that is multicultural is not limited to the curriculum. It encompasses the entire environment of the school. It goes beyond the classroom. Our city, as most cities in this country, is multicultural. In that context it is important that our youth be presented, at every opportunity, with the kind of positive role models and environments that acknowledge and affirm diversity. I also contend that institutional excellence demands a multicultural environment. All of our schools and other institutions that serve our community must be transformed to reflect the multicultural reality of our students, city and nation.

Multicultural education has been described as a "feel good" curriculum, with the entire emphasis placed on self-esteem. The reality is that multicultural education promotes knowledge. Knowledge, not simply of contributions, but also knowledge of heritage, legacy and position of diverse cultures, as a means of fostering respect and arriving at an understanding of those who constitute our global village. Multicultural education fosters self-esteem, but also promotes knowledge. Emphasis on self-esteem should not deflect or divert our attention from the fact that students must be helped to keep up with a knowledge base that is expanding while technological advances make that knowledge increasingly accessible.

Finally, an education that is multicultural is for all students. I would include each of us in that term in some way. All students, not simply students of color, need to be provided an education that is multicultural. All students need to know, understand and respect their own specific cultures as well as that of others. The library is an excellent place to begin or supplement the inquiry.

REFERENCES

1. James A. Banks and Cherry A. Banks, *Multicultural Education: Issues and Perspectives* (Needham Heights, Mass.: Allyn & Bacon, 1993).

2. Sonia Nieto, *Affirming Diversity: The Sociopolitical Context of Multicultural Education* (White Plains, N.Y.: Longman, 1992).

Dividends of Diversity

Alex Boyd

SUMMARY. The advantages of a multicultural society are outlined. The services and programs of the Newark (N.J.) Public Library based upon these advantages are indicated. *[Single or multiple copies of this article are available from The Haworth Document Delivery Service: 1-800-342-9678, 9:00 a.m. - 5:00 p.m. (EST).]*

KEYWORDS. Multiculturalism–advantages, public library response to cultural diversity

A pluralistic society is one in which groups distinctive in ethnic origin, cultural patterns, and religion co-exist; and "multiculturalism," is a commitment to things that reflect or serve the interests of more than one culture. When libraries in a pluralistic society enthusiastically embrace multiculturalism, they receive what I call the Dividends of Diversity. I have identified *seven* such dividends:

First: We benefit from our differences instead of allowing them to divide us.

Second: We experience cultural, social, and intellectual enrichment.

Third: We acknowledge the changing needs of our communities and can, therefore, meet our patrons' diverse needs better.

Alex Boyd, PhD, is Director of the Newark (N.J.) Public Library.

[Haworth co-indexing entry note]: "Dividends of Diversity." Boyd, Alex. Co-published simultaneously in *Public & Access Services Quarterly* (The Haworth Press, Inc.) Vol. 1, No. 3, 1995, pp. 37-39; and: *Mapping Curricular Reform in Library/Information Studies Education: The American Mosaic* (ed: Virgil L. P. Blake) The Haworth Press, Inc., 1995, pp. 37-39. Single or multiple copies of this article are available from The Haworth Document Delivery Service [1-800-342-9678, 9:00 a.m. - 5:00 p.m. (EST)].

Fourth: We recognize and respond intelligently to changes in the workforce.

Fifth: Our differing perspectives strengthen our efforts at problem solving instead of impeding them.

Sixth: We become more creative and adaptable.

Seventh: Individually, we grow in self-understanding and develop a thirst for better understanding of other cultures.

These Dividends of Diversity help us overcome ignorance and indifference. They enable us to use all our skills, experience and commitment to deliver the highest quality of public service. They enable us to explore, communicate, become involved and achieve greater individual fulfillment.

The Newark Public Library, functioning in an extraordinarily pluralistic milieu, wholeheartedly embraces the values of multiculturalism. These values affect every aspect of our work. They instill in us a profound respect for people and their ideas. We are, therefore, able to provide a full scope of services to a diverse community. We bring people *into* the library through cultural events such as exhibitions and public programs and, in doing so, introduce them to other library services.

Some groups, such as African-Americans and Latinos, have been deprived of access to knowledge–deprived of their heritage–kept from searching for their roots. African-Americans lost their history; but after years of struggle they have begun to rediscover their roots. In a small way library outreach programs have helped them do so. Within the Latino community there is no tradition of library use by the general public. Libraries have always been the exclusive province of the elite. When Latinos come to this country, they do not think they will be welcome in libraries. Fortunately, libraries have succeeded in drawing them in through the introduction of programs, services, and collections geared specifically for their needs.

Since 1991 the Newark Public Library has been leading the libraries of New Jersey in their efforts to extend their services to those for whom English is a Second Language. In that year the Newark Public Library was designated as the state's Multilingual

Materials Acquisition Center (MultiMAC). MultiMAC provides a variety of products and services, including booklists, bulk loans, workshops, and translations. MultiMAC develops collections in multiple languages through purchase and through gifts. Dozens of New Jersey libraries have borrowed, and continue to do so, these materials in bulk.

Since its inception MultiMAC has:

- Bought more than 25,000 items in languages such as Chinese, Korean, Vietnamese, Russian, Polish and Spanish.
- Lent more than 10,000 MultiMAC items through the interlibrary loan system.
- Answered more than 700 toll free questions ranging from "Where can I borrow Children's materials in Chinese?" to "Can you recommend a bilingual Spanish/English storyteller?"
- Added more than 750 libraries to its mailing list.
- Held 30 continuing education workshops throughout the state of New Jersey.
- Produced 10 MultiMAC booklists, each ranging from 150 to 350 titles.

Through our multicultural programs we obtain the Dividends of Diversity and these dividends enable us to do what every library must endeavor to do–to serve the community effectively.

Keeping Pace with Changes
in the Curriculum
and in the Student Body

Bernice R. Jones-Trent

SUMMARY. Academic libraries also have a responsibility to broaden resources and services as the student body itself becomes increasingly diverse. At Montclair State College there are procedures in place to ensure that the library provides the resources new curriculum initiatives require. These procedures are outlined in the context of two projects directly related to cultural diversity. *[Single or multiple copies of this article are available from The Haworth Document Delivery Service: 1-800-342-9678, 9:00 a.m. - 5:00 p.m. (EST).]*

KEYWORDS. Multiculturalism and academic libraries, planning for multicultural curriculum

It has become increasingly difficult in light of decreased funding to keep up with collection development commensurate with the needs at a four year, progressive institution. At my institution, Montclair State College, in Upper Montclair, New Jersey, a process is in place that we believe is very effective in managing changes in collection building as dictated by changes in the curriculum and the

Bernice R. Jones-Trent is Director of the Sprague Library, Montclair State University, Upper Montclair, NJ.

[Haworth co-indexing entry note]: "Keeping Pace with Changes in the Curriculum and in the Student Body." Jones-Trent, Bernice R. Co-published simultaneously in *Public & Access Services Quarterly* (The Haworth Press, Inc.) Vol. 1, No. 3, 1995, pp. 41-47; and: *Mapping Curricular Reform in Library/Information Studies Education: The American Mosaic* (ed: Virgil L. P. Blake) The Haworth Press, Inc., 1995, pp. 41-47. Single or multiple copies of this article are available from The Haworth Document Delivery Service [1-800-342-9678, 9:00 a.m. - 5:00 p.m. (EST)].

student body. To illustrate this process I will share with you information related to two recent initiatives and explain how our procedure works to allow us to keep pace with these changes.

The two initiatives are (1) the agenda for teacher education in a democracy project; and (2) multiculturalism at Montclair State College.

THE AGENDA FOR TEACHER EDUCATION IN A DEMOCRACY PROJECT

Two years ago, Montclair State College and the fifteen school districts which constitute its "Clinical Schools Network" were selected as one of the eight original pilot sites in the nation for John Goodlad's "Agenda for Teacher Education in a Democracy" project. The project, which seeks the simultaneous renewal of teacher education and the schools in accordance with a series of presuppositions or "postulates," is directed by the Center for Educational Renewal at the University of Washington. It is sponsored by the Education Commission of the States and the American Association of Colleges for Teacher Education.

Since its inception in 1987, the Clinical Schools Network has been supported by Montclair State College's Institute for Critical Thinking. The Network incorporates the theme "teaching for critical thinking" as a distinctive and consistent vision of teaching and learning upon which to construct a program for both the preparation and professional development of teachers.[1]

Montclair State College's approach to Goodlad's reform agenda was initially organized around the work of three task forces that were charged with respectively addressing (a) the status, prestige, understanding and structure of teacher education at Montclair State College; (b) the collaboration between the College and the public schools, especially the urban schools; and (c) curricular and faculty renewal. Each issue was inspired by a combination of Goodlad's postulates. The task forces were constituted by almost 75 persons who represented the arts and sciences and professional education faculty, administrators from the Clinical Schools Network, undergraduate and graduate certification candidates and the Department of Higher Education.[2]

On the occasion of John Goodlad's visit to Montclair State College last spring (1992) and his commencement address to the graduating class, the chairs of the three task forces reported on the completion of their assignments. In turn, those reports inspired the next phase of their work, which took place during four all day meetings in January, 1993. Fifty persons representing the task force constituencies and two of John Goodlad's senior associates in the Center for Educational Renewal, considered the implementation of the task force recommendations which, for purposes of examination, were organized around five issues. They were: (a) Enrollment Management: Shaping the student body through the admissions process; (b) Restructuring the Teacher Education Program to culminate with a "Professional Year"; (c) Extending the Professional Development School model; (d) Examining the governance of the Teacher Education Program; and (e) Revising curricula in the undergraduate and graduate-level professional education programs to reflect a commitment to teaching for critical thinking, the moral dimensions of teaching, enculturing students into a political and social democracy and promoting stewardship of best practice in the schools.[3]

It is the last issue that impacts the collection development foci of Sprague Library. Curricular revision with respect to critical thinking, moral obligation, enculturation and stewardship, was analyzed with specific reference to the General Education Requirement (GER), major, and professional sequence courses in which those issues are presently emphasized or should be included. Related pedagogical decisions in connection with "best practice" were also discussed, as they are currently being made, for example, in the courses "Teaching for Critical Thinking," "Teacher, School and Society," and "Teaching of Physical Education."[4]

Montclair State College has a long history and tradition of being an institution for the education, training and certification of teachers under the aegis of the School of Professional Studies. The library, naturally, has built a strong collection of materials to support academic pursuits in this field. The process that allows the library to keep pace with related curricular changes is outlined as follows.

Changes to curricula and programs originate and are developed by the academic departments. New courses and program changes also follow this route. The request for a change in a course or a new course begins with the submission of a formal request from the department to the School Dean which is then reviewed and approved or disapproved by the Vice President for Academic Affairs. All such approved changes or new courses are then reviewed by the Collegewide Curriculum Committee and the Graduate Council of which there are several committees that look at various aspects of the request. Upon completion of these reviews and approvals, the Director of Library Services receives a copy of the approved course announcement. This announcement indicates whether the sponsors of the approved course or change noted the level of library collection support. The Director of Library Services reviews each approved course to determine if there is a collection development need.

For each new course, the bibliography for the course is checked against the library's holdings. The Librarian for Acquisitions and Collection Development then completes a report to the Director that indicates the number of items on the bibliography that are in the collection, the number of items not in the collection and a cost estimate for acquiring them and the number of out-of-print titles. Depending upon the point in the library's budgeting cycle, approval is given by the Director of Library Services to acquire the titles now or defer purchasing them to the next budgeting period with top priority. Significant collection needs are brought to the attention of the Deputy Provost/Associate Vice President for Academic Affairs.

For courses reported as deleted from the curriculum, the Librarian for Acquisitions and Collection Development facilitates weeding and recommends withdrawal of these materials that are no longer needed. Faculty members of the affected department review all materials for withdrawal as the last step in the process.

Each program is reviewed for excellence on a three to five year cycle. The Director of Library Services receives the notification of the review and directs the gathering of analytical information on the status of the library's holdings for the department's self study. This self study report is provided to the visiting committee of review. When the committee of review visits to conduct the assessment of the program, the Director of Library services or the Librarian for Acquisitions and Collection Development meets with the visiting committee to review the library component of the self study and to provide access to the collection if requested.

Of Montclair State College's seventy-three majors and interdisciplinary programs, twelve to fifteen are subject to review each year. No program has been denied approval because of insufficient library holdings. The library has, for example, just completed the collection analysis in support of the review of the teacher certification program by NCATE. This program consists of twenty-four disciplines across the entire curriculum and represents a large percentage of the library's collection.

The information from these program reviews and collection analyses is also used for development of the library's materials budget each year.

MULTICULTURALISM AT MONTCLAIR STATE COLLEGE

The second initiative that illustrates the library's methods of keeping pace relates to changes in the composition of the student body. Montclair State College's student body is predominately white but the increase in enrollment of non-white students is significant over the past five years. As the ethnic composition of the 13,000 headcount changes year to year, so does the college's approach to education and student life needs. Montclair State College has been developing a multicultural initiative over the past year which is aimed at generating discussion among faculty, staff and students alike on the exciting, albeit contentious topic of multiculturalism. A long-term goal is to bring multicultural issues to bear on curriculum revision and generally foster a spirit of tolerance and appreciation of ethnic diversity on campus.[5]

According to Professor Anthony Appiah of Harvard University's Department of Afro-American Studies and a recent speaker on multiculturalism at Montclair State College, an affirmative strategy must be incorporated in meeting the purposes of multicultural education. Appiah pointed to the dangers inherent in some multicultural approaches which argue, for example, that we should teach each subculture in the United States "its own history and culture." Such reasoning is harmful in Appiah's opinion because it exacerbates ethnicity and difference, and which, if followed to its logical conclusion, would lead to classes–in itself a patently unconstitutional move. Therefore, according to Appiah, all Americans, and not just African-Americans, for example, ought to be taught about slavery, immigration laws, the underground railroad, and resistance to slavery. Thus, the goal of a multicultural education should be to make all subcultures known to each other. The hard work of multiculturalists lies, in Appiah's opinion, in teaching America's citizens to accept America's diversity, while teaching each of us "the ways and worth of others." Appiah concluded that "if we get this (multiculturalism) right, it will affect everything we teach."[6]

The library has not received any specific directive regarding collection development to support awareness of and the academic pursuits relative to ethnic diversity. However, because it is our nature and our training to monitor and anticipate information seeking habits and needs, we have begun to consider the likely wants and needs of students and faculty who will take different approaches to information gathering and utilization.

For example, for the Paralegal Studies Program which is accredited by the American Bar Association, we have improved our holdings on immigration law this year. For our literature courses, we are acquiring works by and about renowned and lesser known authors of all races and cultures. For our School of Business Program, which is subject to approval by the AACSB, materials are being gathered that demonstrate a global approach to understanding business practices and management principles. Further, we have just completed the second year of a three year commitment to spending as much as $50,000 annually to strengthen the business collection holdings. We have also concentrated selection efforts on obtaining a variety of non-print titles and items that may be utilized by persons involved in presenting programs and seminars on multiculturalism.

Other elements of changes in the student body at Montclair State College that have affected the manner in which we provide library services are the increases in the number of commuting students, older and mature students, graduate students, ESL students, and students from all ethnic groups. These will not be discussed here but would be issues for another time.

In concluding, keeping pace with changes in curricular and the student body is an exciting, scholarly process at Montclair State College and I am proud to say that the library has managed to stay in the forefront with these and other initiatives designed to fulfill the College's mission and vision.

As we build the virtual library, we will have to continue to forge stronger links between the classroom and the library. Our goal is to help students gain the skills they will need most in the next century. These skills include learning how to learn–not only how to access information, but how to grapple with its meanings.[7]

REFERENCES

1. Robert Pines, "Update: The Agenda for Teaching Education in a Democracy Project," *Inquiry: Critical Thinking Across the Disciplines*, 11, 3 (April, 1993), p. 6.

2. Ibid.

3. Ibid.

4. Ibid.

5. Fawzia Afzal-Khan, "Multiculturalism at Montclair State," *Inquiry: Critical Thinking Across the Disciplines*, 11, 3 (April, 1993), p. 11.

6. Ibid.

7. Bernard R. Gifford, "The Learning Society: Libraries Without Books?" *The Chronicle of Higher Education*, April 29, 1992, p. A16.

Who's Out There
and What Do They Want?

Joshua Cohen

SUMMARY. The make-up of communities has been changing at an increased rate, especially the demographic make-up. For libraries the ability to recognize and respond to these changes is crucial. Rather than waiting for a full scale community assessment, techniques such as focus groups, targeted surveys and partnerships can be used to maintain a library's ability to adequately respond to community needs and tailored to work with multicultural populations. *[Single or multiple copies of this article are available from The Haworth Document Delivery Service: 1-800-342-9678, 9:00 a.m. - 5:00 p.m. (EST).]*

KEYWORDS. Community assessment, multicultural, cross-cultural, focus groups, surveys

We are all prisoners of a rigid conception of what is important and what not. We anxiously follow what we suppose to be important, while what we suppose to be unimportant wages guerilla

Joshua Cohen has a Masters Degree in Political Science and Library Science. He is Outreach Consultant for the Mid-Hudson Library System in Poughkeepsie, NY and a member of ALA's Ethnic Materials and Information Exchange Roundtable.

Address correspondence to: Joshua Cohen, 103 Market Street, Poughkeepsie, NY 12601 or Internet MHLSYS2@transit.nyser.net.

[Haworth co-indexing entry note]: "Who's Out There and What Do They Want?" Cohen, Joshua. Co-published simultaneously in *Public & Access Services Quarterly* (The Haworth Press, Inc.) Vol. 1, No. 3, 1995, pp. 49-54; and: *Mapping Curricular Reform in Library/Information Studies Education: The American Mosaic* (ed: Virgil L. P. Blake) The Haworth Press, Inc., 1995, pp. 49-54. Single or multiple copies of this article are available from The Haworth Document Delivery Service [1-800-342-9678, 9:00 a.m. - 5:00 p.m. (EST)].

warfare behind our backs, transforming the world without our knowledge and eventually mounting a surprise attack on us.
      –Milan Kundera, *The Book of Laughter and Forgetting*

Multiculturalism is experiencing backlash. People who wish to deny the reality of what is occurring or who misunderstand the concept of multiculturalism have deemed the movement everything from racist to Balkanization of America. What these critics fail to recognize is what a sampling of almost any community in America reveals: the cultural basis of our communities is being transformed. People wishing to get closer to their heritages, a new cultural group moving into the community, an examination of a variety of cultures for common values, doing business with a variety of cultures are factors causing an increased demand for materials on cultures never before thought of by Americans. People wish to know about folktales, history, customs, celebrations and other facets of world cultures.

The future of libraries will be based on what we can provide. For libraries, product is filling information requests. For users, a successfully filled request without having to resort to Interlibrary Loan is satisfaction. When the library collection cannot meet the patron's needs, most librarians do two things: Inform the patron that the materials they need are available on interlibrary loan, and make a note to purchase some materials that, in the future, would be of value to that patron. Much of a library's collection development is based on what users request rather than what non-users need. This makes sense; after all, if someone is a patron, shouldn't they be ministered to? And if someone is not a patron, why should we care what they want? Let them come in and we will get them what they request. But if we wish to expand the library's image, role, and funding, we must achieve a greater degree of successful patron visits. Achieving this state of perfection is a dream even we library professionals cannot hope to attain, but if we alter the way we do business we can increase the percentage of successful library visits.

How to do this? By having the ability to anticipate our customers needs. In other words, change from passive to active marketing by knowing the community (users and non-users), and knowing what these people wanted. This sounds and can be difficult, but all it requires is good information. And we are information specialists.

The essential component to providing the service your users need is knowing your community. Once you know who is out there, including what they do and how they live, the rest is a matter of deductive logic. The tools needed are on the shelves. Census information provides the age, income, education level, and ethnic breakdown of the community you serve. Regional business guides tell you about the types of industries in your area, and human service directories tell you about agencies. Finally, the newspaper will tell you what types of groups and organizations meet regularly in your community. Once this is pieced together you have begun to market your library. Kay Ann Cassell suggests other, more informal methods of keeping in touch with your community, such as reviewing local newsletters, dropping in on local meetings, contacting community groups at least once a year, reading the minutes of local government and school board meetings, and walking around your community to see what changes are taking place.[1] Being aware of the evolving nature of your community will not only aid your library, but will enhance your role as a community professional.

The next step is determining what information needs these groups have. There are three ways to go about this. Regardless of which method you choose, an important consideration is that these must be ongoing functions. While performing a full-scale community analysis is a good idea once every five years, regular assessment of the community is crucial. These assessments do not have to be as methodologically correct as the full-scale community analyses should be, but can be more of a continual sampling and feedback process that helps you shift direction whenever necessary between those five year periods.

The most stylish of these assessment tools are focus groups. Focus groups are comprised of a selection of people from a target population who are brought together to discuss their opinions. The process for holding a focus group is determining the group you wish to target and inviting representatives of those groups to a meeting. The assumption is that these representatives will provide a description of their needs. This occurs through effective facilitation of the meeting, and here is the problem because focus group facilitation is not as simple as it sounds. At a focus group meeting, three things might happen. One, people will say nothing; two, they will say too much; three, they will say what they think you want to hear. To avoid these probabilities, you need to be trained to lead a focus group, learning how to draw people out, validate comments, and keep the discussion focused. You probably should not lead a group that is discussing your library. To maximize focus groups either hire someone to lead or get training and network with other trainers. Out of this network you can find someone to swap groups with you: you lead the group for their organization and they lead your library group. Option one can be expensive, option two is time consuming. Once you have resolved this problem, focus groups can provide useful information.

Surveys are a second method of finding out what people want. Attempting to survey the entire population is nearly impossible which is why sampling techniques were developed. Sampling is a method of determining the general population's needs by selecting a smaller, more manageable portion of the population and surveying it. The essential issue is how closely the sample groups opinions will mirror that of the larger population. There are several methods of choosing sample groups that suggest representation. The most widely known is *random sampling*. By choosing a sample by chance, theories of probability favor the likelihood that the sample will be representative. There are other more sophisticated methods of sampling, but unless you are willing to hire George Gallup or Lou Harris, they are not an option.

Rather than attempting to sample the entire community, a more feasible, and useful method for libraries is to focus on specific target groups and survey them. By doing this, a librarian will be able to determine the needs of the community with the side benefit of publicizing the library.

Choosing the groups you wish to survey should be subject based. Determine what subjects you need information about. Is the community seeing a rise in small business, or new ethnic groups, or increased interest in the environment? Target one of these groups and design a simple questionnaire that focuses on subject areas. You could list subject areas and ask the respondent to prioritize them or choose the top five. For the best return rate, identify groups or associations of the target group and attend a meeting. By doing this, not only will you find out what the target groups need, but you will also be publicizing the library.

When dealing with cross-cultural groups, it is necessary to consider additional factors which might not be true of a more generic survey. Few countries have the kind of developed library system found in America; for new immigrants the concept of a public library might be strange. A survey form should delineate the purpose and roles of a public library, or an interviewer might have to provide an explanation before beginning the survey. An alternative is to provide a tour of the library before conducting the survey. In this country, being surveyed is a concept we are accustomed to, yet even we are suspicious of surveys. For people from other countries, surveys might be seen as threatening, so clearly stress the anonymity of the response. Finally, when targeting a specific culture it would be prudent to review your plan and survey instrument with an expert or member of that culture to insure that your techniques and questions will not violate any cultural mores.[2]

The survey itself can be written, telephone, or face-to-face. The easiest is telephone, but that factors out people who do not have phones. If conducting a written survey, generally keep it simple. Try to limit it to one page with at least half the questions requiring check-off answers rather than comments. For face to face surveys develop a script that is also simple and uniform. Be sure to have all questions on the script answered before concluding the interview. Whichever method you choose, design the questions with the answers in mind. Know what you wish to find out. Are people using the library? If not, why? What would get them to use the library? While resource needs are important, other factors determine library usage, such as hours and ease of access.

The third technique is to create partnerships with community groups and involve them in needs assessments. Form an advisory committee from targeted groups and solicit input. Also make use of these committees for staff training. Develop cooperative projects and programs with community groups. Take advantage of staff and volunteer connections to link with other groups. Offer to swap speakers or trade volunteers for an agreed upon time period. Find out what resources other agencies possess.[3] These partnerships can provide a wealth of information on what community groups need and what will make them library users and supporters.

All of these ideas are based on the assumption that people actually know what they want. There is no reason to believe this. People generally do not know what their information needs will be in the future. When those needs do occur, they might not think of the library. The analysis of the data generated by these efforts should offer ideas for types of materials. It is the role of the professional librarian to translate these needs into library holdings. This entails interpreting specific answers to a general sense of what will most benefit the respondent. By reviewing new resources and bibliographies, materials selected should provide solutions to the patron's informational requirements.

Attracting non-users to the library is a numbers game: the more hooks out there, the more likely there will be a bite. Each survey a library does reminds people that the library exists. By following the survey with a bibliography of relevant material another hook is thrown in the waters. The fact is that people get mounds of junk in the mail and do not think about it for too long. It is not until they need the information that they start to search, and then it is what is close by that grabs their attention. What libraries have to do is make sure the information is close by when people need it.

Libraries have to reflect their communities while, paradoxically, they must be one step ahead of them. Do this by continually seeking feedback, not the intricate community needs assessments that result in a five-year plan, but ongoing snapshots that become more than the sum of their parts. Change occurs surreptitiously. It is not heralded, but creeps into our consciousness. A new face here, a different request there. By recognizing these changes and responding to them, our value to the community increases and we avoid becoming prisoners of rigid conceptions.

REFERENCES

1. Cassell, Kay Ann, Knowing Your Community and Its Needs, Small Libraries publications-No. 14 American Library Association, 1988.

2. Torres Rita, Assessment of Community Needs, in Scarborough, Katherine, (ed.) Developing Library Collections for California's Emerging Majority, Bay Area Library and Information System, 1990.

3. Van Duyne, Mararet King and Jacobs, Debra, Embracing Diversity: One With One's Bold New Partnerships, in Wilson Library Bulletin, February, 1992.

Spanish Speaking Users
and Their Communities:
A Librarian's Response

Katharine M. Breen

SUMMARY. Originally presented to a conference on curriculum reform for library science faculties, this article reflects on how public librarians can assist new Spanish speaking users. Based on various career involvements with Latino communities, the author covers aspects of library outreach, initial user contact, introduction to and tour of the public library; points to a gap between traditional library service and non-users and offers suggestions that will encourage return visits by new users. *[Single or multiple copies of this article are available from The Haworth Document Delivery Service: 1-800-342-9678, 9:00 a.m. - 5:00 p.m. (EST).]*

KEYWORDS. Spanish speaking users, information needs, non-users, coping skills, Spanish language

At the outset it should be noted that these are the reflections of a non-Latina librarian, one who sees the Latino community from the outside and the library from the inside; hence the subtitle.

Katharine M. Breen holds an MA in Spanish and Secondary Education from Middlebury College, VT and an MLS from Queens College (CUNY) NY. She is Coping Skills Coordinator with the New Americans Program, Queens Borough Public Library, Queens, NY. She is a member of the American Library Association; and REFORMA, National Association to Promote Library Services to the Spanish Speaking.

[Haworth co-indexing entry note]: "Spanish Speaking Users and Their Communities: A Librarian's Response." Breen, Katharine M. Co-published simultaneously in *Public & Access Services Quarterly* (The Haworth Press, Inc.) Vol. 1, No. 3, 1995, pp. 55-61; and: *Mapping Curricular Reform in Library/ Information Studies Education: The American Mosaic* (ed: Virgil L. P. Blake) The Haworth Press, Inc., 1995, pp. 55-61. Single or multiple copies of this article are available from The Haworth Document Delivery Service [1-800-342-9678, 9:00 a.m. - 5:00 p.m. (EST)].

55

The perspective with which I come to this topic began taking shape in the 1960s, when I was a teenager. I chose to study Spanish rather than French in high school because it would be more practical in relating to the new immigrants in my neighborhood. College and graduate school prepared me to be a teacher of Spanish. Short visits to Central America and work as a community organizer with various Latino communities in New York further developed my ease in speaking the language.

I was drawn to the service aspect of my second language; I preferred using Spanish to teach literacy and high school equivalency to Latinos, rather than to teach the language to Anglos. However, I did enjoy teaching Spanish to adults who were preparing to work within the Latino community. With time, I found that my second language capability carried with it a distinct spirit; the words flowed freely, as if I had inherited an additional dimension of personality, and with it an openness to Spanish speaking people.

Initially, it was this persona that felt the attraction to work with the Queens Borough Public Library. In 1986 when the New Americans Program created a coordinator position for its new coping skills component, the focus of which was to assist new immigrants, it was the opportunity for outreach to Latinos that beckoned me most strongly.

What shapes the particular views presented here is this personal history. What I offer is obvious to me, and I have often assumed it to be self-evident. But maybe it is obvious only to those who have struggled with learning a second language. My remarks are intended as an invitation to reconsider appropriate ways to serve non-user groups, rather than as a list of solutions to problems.

My work at the Queens library was propelled and animated by my experience with Latino communities. I found that this experience provided me with a bridge to other language communities. Having established a rapport with one community, I was able to generalize what I learned and approach others. I learned that people newly arrived in this country share certain basic needs for orientation. Immigrants, despite the differences of their countries of origin, have a lot in common.

When I began working with the New Americans Program, the initial task was to get the word out to newcomers that the library was there, ready to respond to their information needs. The method created to do this was coping skills workshops to be presented by professionals in the languages of the largest immigrant groups of Queens: Spanish, Chinese and Korean. These sessions would offer orientations to some facet of living in this country that was directly affecting their lives, and would provide basic information often hard to get through other sources.

As a rule of thumb, I planned programs on practical topics that might have wide appeal. My approach was to consider the information needs of newcomers, find out the answers, then develop the programs with appropriate supports that would best present the topics. Some examples of successful programs are: tenant-landlord law, how to start a small business, orientations on how the public schools function, parenting skills like how to help your child learn or how to talk with your teenager, and orientations on immigrants rights.

The success of these sessions in providing information is measured in direct proportion to the utility of the information. Newcomers who attend a session come with a question and expect an answer. If the presenter strays too far into theory, wandering away from the application of the topic to this particular time, place and situation, a participant's question or comment will call attention to the real needs. As an example, a recent program on stress management evoked the comment, "But I thought you would give us some exercises to do right now for stress reduction."

Similarly, a program might have the appearance of success; it might attract two hundred enthusiastic participants. Yet, if it provides little more than a sense of elation (not to be disparaged) and is devoid of informative data and follow-up resources, its enduring value for the new immigrant is negligible.

At the beginning of each session a bilingual librarian introduces participants to the variety of library services. Most newcomers have had no experience of a public library. It often comes as a great surprise that one can borrow books. Many think that the books are for sale!

The treasures of the public library are out of reach for most newcomers, not purposely so, but because there is a gap of experience on the part of both, the library and the newcomer. The gap is one of contrasts: the relative ease with which a librarian learns the way things are and how things function, as contrasted with the discomfort a newcomer may feel with not knowing and not knowing how to find out. This discomfort is an experience shared by all library newcomers, those born in this country and those from abroad.

My own experience might account for my solidarity with newcomers. The gap in understanding how the library works is something I felt when I began to study library science after having worked for the library as program coordinator for six years (I earned an MLS degree one year ago). In preparing my first reference assignment, the frustration I felt was no pretense or role-play as I navigated my way as a newcomer in the library. I was often lost. I kept trying to get behind the strange language of librarians, beyond what they assumed I already knew, having seen me around for years. Following each frustration I queried, "If I am having such difficulty navigating, how can a newcomer with little if any fluency in English, ever learn how things work?" The rational question after my rude awakening, now that I have learned to maneuver, is, "Who will tell the people?"

While in library school I began working one day a week as a reference librarian; I continue this still, because I enjoy direct contact with the users. My recent experiences as a student have sensitized me to the frustrations one might feel as a newcomer to the library. Nevertheless, when under pressure, I catch myself giving a user the pat answers others had once given me. But more often I err to the other extreme, and use a walk-through or hands-on approach, unwilling to lose to frustration even one of the uninitiated.

If the user begins by saying, "I've never been here before," or something similar, it is rather easy to give appropriate assistance. But when, as is most often the case, a user's inquiry is not so prefaced, and one answers with library vocabulary, without confirming that there has been comprehension, the newcomer will probably just go away, wondering if the words will ever make sense. That is what I have done.

Native speakers of Spanish come from more than twenty nations; the language is common to all, but its use in each country has its particular characteristics. In addition, characteristics of gender, age, socio-economic background, education and experience, combine to form the identity of each Latino person, making it impossible, when referring to people as Spanish, Hispanic or Latino, to make any general assumptions. And this includes the assumption that they speak Spanish, since many U.S. born children of immigrants prefer English as their primary language, and put aside the language of their parents. Many of my observations about the new Spanish speaking user can be applied to any new user group, regardless of language facility or country of origin. For present purposes, I am recalling specific situations with Spanish speaking individuals in a library setting.

Few adult Latinos come to this country already familiar with the phenomenon we call the public library. Immigrants with a university education may have used a research library in their country. But what we know as a public library is not common in the Americas to the South. The predominant response from an audience, having listened to an introduction to library services, is one of amazement. They never knew or dreamed of the fabulous realm that we take for granted.

Often adult non-users are escorted to the library for the first time by their children, either for a program or a school assignment. Traditional library services such as picture-book hour and story-time can help immigrant children socialize and learn the English language in ways their parents cannot provide. Listening to songs and stories on tape can be a family affair and provide incidental learning in the home for adults and older children who may be eavesdropping.

It is from this initial point of contact that the librarian can introduce adults to the larger library, all the while understanding that they will probably not ask for what they really want. Browsing is the preferred strategy for most. The parent who assists a child in completing a school assignment in the children's room might not know, and would never dream of asking about, the extensive Spanish collection available to borrowers: books, magazines, cassettes, CD's, and videos. Librarians are aware that various language collections exist; new immigrants, who are also new users, have no idea of their existence, unless someone shows them.

If it is known that a family can speak English, a librarian might judge there to be no need for Spanish language materials. But it is a mistake to think that because one speaks English one's reading preferences are all in the English language. I ask myself how much I have read lately in Spanish, since I speak Spanish. One's native language is a resource that is never displaced by a second language, notwithstanding the level of fluency. It is the intimacy of a first language that keeps individuals connected to their roots and that can broaden their approach to life.

When the Latino user does ask a question, generally it is preceded with, "Perdone la molestia," "Excuse me for bothering you." I have seen new users wander off course browsing when actually they are looking for a specific book, call number in hand. Dewey decimals mean nothing to those who have not been informed about the underlying organization of the library. Words common to librarians, like stacks, index, fiche, microfilm, and all the expressions within the realm of technology, sound like code to the uninitiated. When assisting a user use library terminology sparingly. Give an English lesson not a library science lesson. The user will be better served and might even return.

A steady source of potential users is English as a second language classes. The class that visits the local library would greatly benefit from a customized tour, bilingual if possible, that connects them with practical information they can use on a later visit. Were they to be shown the library in the same manner as an American high school class, most of the content would remain incomprehensible. Among the aspects of library service that are new to most immigrants are such basics as the catalog, borrowing or charging books, circulating and reference copies, reference questions, indexes, the various media, and computer searches.

The pressing information needs of newcomers, concern management of daily life. Some absolutes for an ESL library tour are: language collections, native language encyclopedias and bilingual dictionaries, ESL books, tapes and videos, youth services, job information resources, test preparation books (including citizenship), resumé samples, and information on higher education, newspapers and magazines, road maps, and current topics in the vertical file. Tours that are participatory, that is, responsive to the inquiries of the students, can serve as sensitivity training for the librarian-guide as well. The guide needs only to mentally step out of the familiar and walk into the library, as if for the first time, in order to simplify the new immigrant's entry.

For many immigrants, Central Americans for example, the circumstances which motivated their move to this country are related to great duress. Often their lives in the U.S. are prolonged struggles for survival and they have little opportunity for library leisure. Yet, the library has the very services that might help them progress in their new life and feel supported culturally. Among the library activities that can contribute to this sense of belonging are concerts of Latin music and dance, English classes, educational and vocational guidance, books, music and videos by native authors, composers and directors, Spanish newspapers, magazines and foto-novelas, and a postage paid Spanish books-by-mail service with no library card required.

Librarians know and enjoy the library as a treasure trove of information. Who will tell the nonusers? From the hints provided by the new immigrant, the sensitive librarian can determine what additional sources of information might be helpful, and then give them suggestions. Gratitude will be the overwhelming response.

Beyond Quality Services

Elizabeth S. Hsu

SUMMARY. Queens Borough of New York City is the most culturally diverse community in America. The New Americans Project
was established to meet the unique needs of this community. The focus here is the Asian American community. The procedures for ensuring appropriate materials for the Chinese and Korean communities are detailed. *[Single or multiple copies of this article are available
from The Haworth Document Delivery Service: 1-800-342-9678, 9:00
a.m. - 5:00 p.m. (EST).]*

KEYWORDS. New Americans Project (Queens Borough Public
Library), collection development, library services to Chinese, library
services to Koreans

Good afternoon!

Several years ago when I invited some non-Chinese friends over
for dinner I said "Come at 6 p.m.," without specifying "for dinner." They had dinner at home before coming over and were sur-
prised to find an eight-course gourmet meal waiting for them. I said,
"6 p.m. implies dinner." They disagreed. I couldn't get over the
shock and disappointment for a long, long time! Cultural differences may result in serious consequences, in addition to embarrass-

Elizabeth S. Hsu is affiliated with the Queens Borough Public Library, New
Americans Project, Jamaica, NY.

[Haworth co-indexing entry note]: "Beyond Quality Services." Hsu, Elizabeth S. Co-published
simultaneously in *Public & Access Services Quarterly* (The Haworth Press, Inc.) Vol. 1, No. 3, 1995,
pp. 63-69; and: *Mapping Curricular Reform in Library/Information Studies Education: The American
Mosaic* (ed: Virgil L. P. Blake) The Haworth Press, Inc., 1995, pp. 63-69. Single or multiple copies of
this article are available from The Haworth Document Delivery Service [1-800-342-9678, 9:00 a.m. -
5:00 p.m. (EST).]

ment! Understanding different people, different countries and different cultures has become a necessity in today's society! A few days ago when I unexpectedly received an E-Mail from a colleague in Barcelona, I knew the day was not far off when I would be communicating with people all over the world on video screens. I felt both excited and terrified. Excited, because our progress doesn't seem to be controlled by time and space any more! Terrified, because as computers and other technology telescope the world, they inadvertently magnify our differences, and at a rate too rapid for us to cope with! The need for proper interaction among the peoples of the world makes it necessary to redefine our roles and responsibilities and to perform accordingly. Proper interaction begins at home. By the year 2000, minority groups will account for 35% of America's population. Haven't we suffered enough from racial tension? As informational professionals in today's multicultural environment, are we equipped with the resources to provide information from different perspectives? I'm sure most of us share the same vision of multi-culturalism, resource sharing and quality service. *But, IS QUALITY SERVICE ALL WE ARE HERE FOR?*

I'm from the New Americans Program, NAP for short, of the Queens Borough Public Library.

Queens Library has had the highest circulation of any city library system in the country since 1986. Queens has nearly two million people. Three out of ten are immigrants and four out of ten speak a language other than English at home. Queens immigrants represent more than 100 countries and 120 languages. To help the Queens Library fulfill its mission to provide quality service to all Queens residents, the New Americans Program was initiated in 1977, and is now established as one of the largest programs of its kind in the country. NAP has been cited as a model in serving ethnic populations by ALA, the California State Library, and the National Library of Canada.

NAP extends library services to immigrants whose native language is not English and helps them adjust to American life. NAP has an office staff of six professionals and two clerks and a field staff of twenty-four ESL teachers.

- Through NAP, Queens Library is a major provider of free English-as-a-Second-Language (ESL) classes. During the last fiscal year, NAP offered 72 classes, attended by 2,600 adult students representing 80 countries and 50 languages.
- During this period, NAP not only maintained and expanded large Chinese, Spanish and Korean collections in 28 branches, but also purchased materials in 10 other languages for branch collections.
- NAP also operates a books-by-mail service for Queens residents in seven languages and presents programs to celebrate the cultures of various ethnic groups; as well as coping skills programs in immigrant languages to help newcomers adjust to American life. Finally, NAP has published a "Queens Directory of Immigrant Serving Agencies" and maintains a database of immigrant-serving agencies, which staff use to refer callers to a wide range of local services offered either bilingually or in immigrant languages.

Of the 19 Asian American nationalities and ethnic groups, the six major ones in N.Y. in terms of population are Chinese, Indians, Koreans, Filipinos, Japanese and Vietnamese. Of the five boroughs of New York City, Queens has the largest number of Asians, with Chinese and Korean immigration showing the largest increases over the last decade.

The Chinese and Korean language collections at the Queens Borough Public Library are among *the largest circulating collections* for the *general public* in the United States in these languages.

Now, due to the time limit, I'll tell you very briefly how we developed these two collections, and then give you some tips on collection development for Asian Americans in general. As much as possible, I'll leave statistics and other boring stuff to the handouts.

The Chinese population of Queens, according to the latest census, is over 90,000. The main countries of origin are Taiwan, China, Hong Kong, and the SE Asian countries. In 1988, following the success of Queens Library's Spanish language collection program, the Library launched the Ni Hao campaign to meet the borough's growing demand for Chinese materials. "Ni Hao" means "greetings" in Chinese. The goal of the program is to build well-rounded collections with emphasis on publications of modern literature by best selling authors from the 1920s through the present. We build collections not only to meet the changing needs of the community, but also to promote awareness and usage of library facilities, programs and services. Our services have attracted new customers for our ethnic collections, which, in turn, have attracted new customers for our services. Both services and collections are also superb PR tools, which have greatly raised the library's profile in the community.

During the past five years, NAP has placed Chinese collections, totalling 80,000 items in Central and twenty-eight branches with a total budget of nearly $721,000.

Based on our survey findings, circulation patterns of branches, and direct communication with customers and library staff, we divide the Ni Hao libraries into three different categories and distribute resources accordingly. Materials include books, magazines and newspapers, audio and video cassettes, and CDs. Video tapes and CDs are limited to five branches. All materials are selected from local stores by experienced and knowledgeable Chinese librarians from around the system as well as NAP staff. The only disadvantage of local ordering is that we are subject to dealer's selection preferences. At least 90% of adult books and all video cassettes are cataloged. One of our selection criteria is to ensure that materials from the three main regions of emigration, Taiwan, China and Hong Kong, are represented in fair proportion. A balanced selection of items in the Mandarin and Cantonese dialects is also considered in selecting audio and video cassettes. On average, the entire Ni Hao collections circulate at least once a month in the most heavily used branches; popular books may circulate 14-25 times a year, popular magazines, four times a month. We have greatly expanded and fine-tuned the Chinese collections based on local needs as well as circulation patterns. We transfer materials among branches to ensure maximum utilization. The main features of the Ni Hao collections are:

- All collections are developed based on the reading preferences of the communities, and the expert recommendations of our Chinese staff.
- Our periodical subscriptions list, containing 137 magazines and 6 newspapers, is comprehensive in terms of scope, and re-

flects diversity and balance in terms of the three major source countries of immigration, and in terms of political viewpoint. They provide an important source of information and recreation for our customers as well as circulation for the library.

- Standing orders have made it possible for hot, popular items to be placed on the shelves of our Ni Hao branches as soon as they become available.
- Through careful weeding and merchandising, we have maximized our investment. Branches with solid Ni Hao collections have all enjoyed a tremendous circulation increase.

Now how did we build our Korean language collections?

More than 90% of the Koreans in the U.S. arrived after 1970; a majority of the Koreans in Queens arrived after 1980. Now about one million Koreans live in the U.S., more than 200,000 of them in the New York area. Close to 74,000 Koreans live in Queens.

During the 80s NAP purchased some 5,000 volumes of Korean books for ten branches. Circulation was modest: average circulation per title was, at most, six times a year.

In 1989 things began to change. Customers and managers requested Korean books more frequently.

In 1991 we received an LSCA grant of nearly $13,000 to conduct a pilot Korean program. We placed nearly identical collections of books, audio cassettes and magazines in two branch libraries.

We used the pilot program to test our assumptions about Korean collection building. We believed that Korean communities had become aware enough of the Library to use up-to-date collections on a regular basis; that readers were interested in a wide variety of fiction and non-fiction; and that cataloging everything would facilitate collection building and access to collections.

Our assumptions were proved by the Korean pilot project: circulation is near maximum capacity; every category of fiction and non-fiction–and nearly every title–circulates equally well.

In 1992 we received a second LSCA grant and used $58,000 of the award to expand Korean collections.

We buy off the shelf from Koryo bookstore in Manhattan and Chongro bookstore in Flushing, two of the largest Korean booksellers on the East coast. The owners of both stores visit Korea every two or three months to select new titles. Both are knowledgeable about Korean literature and publishing. Nevertheless, our selection is limited by their tastes and those of their customers; there are many books published in Korea that we've never seen.

During the past two years, we have placed a total of more than 10,000 items in ten branches. A majority of items in all ten collections circulate once a month. The Korean community has discovered QBPL! Korean collection development is off to a very promising start.

Now let's move on from specific language collections to some general tips on ethnic materials development for Asian Americans.

1. It's important to base a collection development project on a library's specific mission, and to have collection development principles, guidelines and policies. It's equally important to conduct ongoing assessment of the changing information needs of the intended clientele of the community the library serves, so that appropriate and adequate collections with the right focus and features can be developed and maintained.

2. Short term and long term planning on budgeting, acquisition, cataloging, resource distribution, and personnel, as well as regular evaluation and proper documentation of the collection development process will ensure continuity and success.

3. Currently, many library systems are still using different on-line public catalog systems which do not interface with RLIN/CJK system and procedures. Only when libraries and publishers share a standardized cataloging system, can we talk about true bibliographic control and access. We can then accomplish on-line search, price comparison, ordering without unwanted duplication, etc. Bilingual invoices can then become a reality for all.

5. Ethnic collections should include materials both for circulation and reference. They should be in ethnic language, in English, and in bilingual format so as to benefit all readers.

6. Be creative in acquiring materials–auctions, book fairs, donations, special grants, and exchanges should all be explored.

7. Material selection tools, such as Chinese and Korean BIP in bilingual format, and standardized book reviews are badly needed, along with currently available, annotated dealers' catalogues.

8. Finally, recruitment and placement of bilingual staff to develop and maintain ethnic collections will facilitate and maximize the use of collections.

Before you all fall asleep, or worse, walk out on me, I'd like to stress that collection development can be rewarding, too. Last week, as I was conducting my annual evaluation of a Chinese collection in a branch, a Chinese mother stood next to me browsing the shelves. When I asked her opinion of the collection, she expressed complete satisfaction and offered her appreciation to the Queens Library and the U.S. government. Then she turned and said: "I wonder whether our government is doing the same for foreigners in Taiwan!"

Her comment really opened my eyes! While I was looking down at my collections in Queens, she was looking halfway around the world! She's looking beyond the present moment. Shouldn't we be doing the same? A generation ago, who was thinking about large Asian language collections for public libraries? As we talk about collection development and quality service, is there anything else we are overlooking before we reach the year 2000? Does her question reveal the need for global information service? Do we have the resources for that? Are we ready for the challenge–a joint venture to accomplish everything that may be asked of us in today's global community? What do you think? Thank you and let me hear your suggestions.

Multiculturalism and Technology in the Academic Library

Mario A. Charles

SUMMARY. The impact of controversial subjects and information technology on research in academic libraries is the subject of this essay. The debates surrounding multiculturalism, problems encountered during information retrieval and instruction of patrons involved in scholarly pursuits illustrate the changes occurring in contemporary libraries. The article also discusses user perceptions of database structures, the importance of librarians remaining sensitive to the public, and confirms the need for service oriented professionals in academic libraries. *[Single or multiple copies of this article are available from The Haworth Document Delivery Service: 1-800-342-9678, 9:00 a.m. - 5:00 p.m. (EST).]*

KEYWORDS. Multiculturalism and database searching, information retrieval systems, multiculturalism and searchers, education for searchers

The multicultural debate taking place on many college campuses challenges a tradition of educational conservatism. Both scholarly and political discussions surround this issue and influence academic librarians and, at times, even affect how they organize and retrieve information in the electronic library environment. A recent article on multiculturalism by Kessler-Harris (1992) states:

Mario A. Charles is affiliated with the Reference Department, Baruch College, City University of New York.

[Haworth co-indexing entry note]: "Multiculturalism and Technology in the Academic Library." Charles, Mario A. Co-published simultaneously in *Public & Access Services Quarterly* (The Haworth Press, Inc.) Vol. 1, No. 3, 1995, pp. 71-83; and: *Mapping Curricular Reform in Library/Information Studies Education: The American Mosaic* (ed: Virgil L. P. Blake) The Haworth Press, Inc., 1995, pp. 71-83. Single or multiple copies of this article are available from The Haworth Document Delivery Service [1-800-342-9678, 9:00 a.m. - 5:00 p.m. (EST)].

At the heart of the recent controversy over multiculturalism lies a concern for what constitutes America. To opponents of multiculturalism, America is intimately tied to ideas about the nature of Western civilization and the particular humanistic values, such as individual freedom and tolerance, that it is said to represent. As advocates of multiculturalism attempt to incorporate into the curriculum and the campus environment the wide range of cultures that coexist in the United States, critics counter that multicultural courses will displace traditional subjects, depriving students of instruction in the heritage of Western democracy. (p. 1)

Discourse on multiculturalism is sustained in scholarship which contrasts pluralistic and multicultural education and examines their impact on the psyche of students (Gambino, 1992). Other discussions question the value of traditional literature and recommend alternative non-Western sources (D'Souza, 1991). Some articles describe faculty who resign after learning that their view of multiculturalism conflicts with the administrations (Wong, 1991). Titles such as "The Opening of the American Mind" (Lee, 1991); and "What Should We Teach our Children About American History: An interview with Arthur Schlesinger Jr.," (Smoler, 1992) represent many of the issues at the heart of the present debate in the academic community and elsewhere. Schlesinger (1991) writes of a "militant multiculturalism" (p. 14) and its cadre of supporters poised to undermine the present Eurocentric curriculum and replace it with an Afrocentric course of study. Universities and colleges will continue to discuss this controversial issue utilizing numerous articles to support their stance on the issue. Academic libraries, however, can not wait for the outcome of scholarly discussions before classifying controversial subjects. They must continue to fulfill their mission to educate, organize, and provide access to past and present material. Catalogers must assign subject headings even if arguments influence them. The following example illustrates how the cataloging of a subject can impact on a patrons research.

A student searching for information on Chicanos used "Latino" as a subject heading and discovered it was cross-referenced to "Hispanics." After examining the cross-references listed under "Hispanics" the student asked for assistance. She wondered why Mexican Americans (Chicanos) were not listed under "Hispanics" while Puerto Ricans and other Spanish speaking people were. At the reference desk the librarian attempted to explain the cataloging rules without much success. In the database "Hispanic," which was assigned according to Library of Congress rules, did not include Chicanos in its list of sub-headings. The student laughed [sic] at the way the subject was classified. She said Chicanos spoke Spanish and that information about them should be found under "Latinos" or "Hispanics." She had a point since, omitting Chicanos raises valid questions about the cataloging of material about Spanish speaking people.

Librarians must remain sensitive to the complexities of information retrieval, of the external influences on the classification of library resources, and how this classification influences researchers. Students and other users must also learn to think about the various ways a subject could be cataloged.

Many catalogers for electronic indexes depend on personal knowledge and nonstandardized classification schemes to assign subject headings. They do not implement widely accepted cataloging rules, such as Library of Congress subject headings, when they codify information. This type of index lacks authority control which makes it difficult to use as a research tool. According to some electronic index salespersons researchers should exercise their "intuition" when they encounter this kind of database. Library patrons often compound existing information retrieval problems when they choose search terms. They do not prepare search strategies and count on their concept of a subject to select search terms which often result in useless searches. Academic librarians often overhear students complaining about this dilemma.

An African-American student who did not have much success in locating information on her culture was told to use the term "Negro" when looking for historical data. She asked the reference librarian when it was appropriate to use the term. After the librarian explained the difference in the index between "Black," "Negro," and "African-American" the student referred to herself as black and said she began her research with this phrase. She also objected to "Negro" because of its historical association with discrimination against blacks. Personal politics and undeveloped research strategy could have prevented this student from finding the information she sought.

Locating book reviews, scholarly articles, or statistical data in on-line and off-line indexes is not a simple task for many researchers. Many library patrons request professional assistance when faced with the maze of electronic indexes found in some academic libraries. They ask librarians to define the contents of an index, teach command language, or for advice on how to design research strategy. Researchers have the option of reviewing help screens but most, especially students, do not have the time nor the inclination to read this user friendly text; they want their citations immediately. Although help screens teach rudimentary skills, they are incapable of teaching the critical thinking that is necessary to the development of effective research strategies. Until researchers exercise critical thinking, a higher order thought process, they will remain unaware of the idiosyncracies of different databases and experience fruitless searches.

> After spending some time in the library an Asian student asked for assistance at the reference desk. He explained he was fulfilling a class assignment on multiculturalism and looking for information about his culture. He was told to key in "China–History" as a subject heading and directed to the automated periodicals index for articles. He was unsatisfied with the librarians response since this was the terminology he had used to search the index. The student explained he was American born Chinese (ABC) and should not be confused with someone born in China. The librarian suggested that "Chinese–Americans" was the subject heading he should use for his research after listening to the student. This researcher did not think about his subject critically.

This search and the other examples of student research took place in the library at Baruch College of the City University of New York (CUNY). Students were introduced to "and" the boolean connector and warned about the inconsistencies between database subject headings. They were also encouraged to use critical thinking skills and to design alternative research strategies that were adaptable for different databases.

As early as 1880 Otis Hall Robinson spoke of the importance of students learning how to use the library (Hardesty, 1992). Librarians persist in this goal by teaching information retrieval in informal and formal settings which enables patrons to be lifelong learners.

Today, however, the acquisition of information retrieval systems by public service units in academic libraries across the country alienates many students, faculty and other library users. They find technology an obstacle to research and interpret the computer clicks and beeps as threats from a high-tech environment. Other patrons welcome automation and have insight into the shifting role of libraries. They recognize the role of librarians is no longer confined to that of "custodians of shelves of books," (Holderness, 1992, p. 22). They view CD-ROMs and their ability to print abstracts of articles as invaluable tools. Yes, the electronic index is impressive, but there is another, less glamorous, aspect of the system that must be considered.

A look at subject searches on multiculturalism in some electronic indexes, is illustrative of many of its problems. The following searches took place at the Baruch College Library of the City University of New York (CUNY), during 1991 and 1992. In addition to printed indexes there were ten CD-ROMs on a LAN (local area network) serving seven work stations, four terminals indexing and abstracting newspapers and magazine articles, and nine CUNY+ (City University of New York Online Catalog) OPAC (online public access catalogs) terminals indexing books and periodicals, located in the reference area. Additional information retrieval systems consisted of the United States Census data, Dow Jones Newspaper Index and a WordCruncher terminal. Cuny+s DPAC conformed to Library of Congress cataloging standards the other databases did not. This array of machines often overwhelmed the students and faculty who came to the library to do research. Most library patrons had no idea where to begin to look for a book in this electronic environment. They were not aware that a subject search for books on multiculturalism in DPAC results in the following display or of the following dissimilarity between databases.

```
Search Request: S=MULTICULTURALISM                          DPAC
Search Results: 1 Entry Found                       Subject Index

vvvvvvvvvvvvvvvvvvvvvvvvvvvvvvvvvvvvvvvvvvvvvvvvvvvvvvvvvvvvvvvvv


        MULTICULTURALISM

   1    *Search Under: PLURALISM SOCIAL SCIENCES




vvvvvvvvvvvvvvvvvvvvvvvvvvvvvvvvvvvvvvvvvvvvvvvvvvvvvvvvvvvvvvvvv
```

"Multiculturalism" is cross indexed to "Pluralism–Social Sciences." It is interesting to note that in 1991, titles under multiculturalism pertained to African-Americans. Since then new entries have been introduced possibly as a result of the controversy over the initial cataloging of materials which only pertained to African-Americans under multiculturalism. It is apparent, in this example, that locating information on a controversial topic depends on individual interpretations of the topic, how catalogers assign subject headings, and on how academic arguments can influence the cataloging of a subject.

A look at the "see" reference, "Pluralism–Social Sciences" reveals "see also" references to "Biculturalism" and "Ethnicity." The first title is *America Without Ethnicity* (the symbols at the end of the record indicate different locations for the title). The main subject of this book is "Pluralism," the next is "United States–Race Relations."

```
Search Request: S=PLURALISM SOCIAL SCIENCES                    DPAC
Search Results: 690 Entries Found                     Subject Index
VVVVVVVVVVVVVVVVVVVVVVVVVVVVVVVVVVVVVVVVVVVVVVVVVVVVVVVVVVVVVVVV

        PLURALISM SOCIAL SCIENCES
          *Search Also Under:

   1    BICULTURALISM
   2    ETHNICITY


        PLURALISM SOCIAL SCIENCES
   3    AMERICA WITHOUT ETHNICITY  [1981]    (BB)
   4    AMERICA WITHOUT ETHNICITY  [1981]    (BC)
   5    AMERICA WITHOUT ETHNICITY  [1981]    (HC)
   6    AMERICA WITHOUT ETHNICITY  [1981]    (JJ)
   7    AMERICA WITHOUT ETHNICITY  [1981]    (LE)
   8    AMERICA WITHOUT ETHNICITY  [1981]    (QC)
   9    AMERICA WITHOUT ETHNICITY  [1981]    (SI)
  10    AMERICAN DEMOCRATIC THEORY PLURALISM AND ITS [1978]  (BB)
  11    AMERICAN DEMOCRATIC THEORY PLURALISM AND ITS [1978]  (BC)

VVVVVVVVVVVVVVVVVVVVVVVVVVVVVVVVVVVVVVVVVVVVVVVVVVVVVVVVVVVVVVVV

COMMANDS:         Type line # to see individual record

                  F   Forward     H   Help
O   Other Options  G   Guide

NEXT COMMAND:
```

```
Search Request: S=PLURALISM SOCIAL SCIENCES                    DPAC
BOOK    Record 3 of 690 Entries Found                    Brief View
VVVVVVVVVVVVVVVVVVVVVVVVVVVVVVVVVVVVVVVVVVVVVVVVVVVVVVVVVVVVVVVV

Author:        Morgan, Gordon D.

Title:         America without ethnicity

Publisher:     Port Washington, N .Y.: Kennikat Press, 1981.

Subjects:      Pluralism (Social Sciences)
               Minorities vv United States
               United Statates vv Ethnic Relations
               United States vv Race relations
VVVVVVVVVVVVVVVVVVVVVVVVVVVVVVVVVVVVVVVVVVVVVVVVVVVVVVVVVVVVVVVV
       LOCATION:          CALL NUMBER          STATUS:
1.     Baruch Stacks 7th  E184.A1  M673        Not Checked Out
       Floor
VVVVVVVVVVVVVVVVVVVVVVVVVVVVVVVVVVVVVVVVVVVVVVVVVVVVVVVVVVVVVVVV
COMMANDS:                 LO  Long View    I  Index
                          N   Next Record  G  Guide
0 Other Options           P  Previous Record H  Help

NEXT COMMAND:
```

In DPAC professional catalogers insure uniformity between entries by maintaining Library of Congress cataloging standards. This does not carry over to the other electronic indexes. For example, a subject search for information on multiculturalism at the same CUNY+ terminal but in DWIL the periodicals index results in the following display.

```
Search Request: S=MULTICULTURALISM          OCOB6D66POS@DWIL
Search Results: 29 Entries Found                Subject Index
VVVVVVVVVVVVVVVVVVVVVVVVVVVVVVVVVVVVVVVVVVVVVVVVVVVVVVVVVVVVVV
       MULTICULTURALISM
   1   BLENDERS  [1992]     (RD)
   2   CENTRAL CHALLENGE FOR MUSEUMS TODAY MAY BE T   [1992]   (RD)
   3   CRACKING THE CULTURAL CONSENSUS      [1991]    (RD)
   4   DEAD ASIAN MALE CONFUCIUS AND MULTICULTURALI   [1992]   (RD)
```

```
  5  DROWNING IN THE MELTING POT       [1992]      (RD)

  6  E PLURIBUS UNUM      [1991]      (RD)

  7  FOCUS ON THE MULTICULTURAL WORKPLACE      [1992]      (RD)

  8  FORBIDDEN TOPIC      [1992]      (RD)

  9  FRAYING OF AMERICA      [1992]      (RD)

 10  GIVE GET OR GET OFF      [1993]      (RD)

 11  GREAT HALL OF BACTERIA      [1992]      (RD)

 12  MULTICULTURALISM AND ME      [1992]      (RD)

 13  NATION OF DISCONTENTS      [1992]      (RD)

 14  ON THE IMPORTANCE OF BEING TRIBAL AND THE PR      [1992]    (RD)
VVVVVVVVVVVVVVVVVVVVVVVVVV Continued on next screen VVVVVVVVVVVVVVVVVVVVVVVVV
COMMANDS:                Type Line # to see individual record
                         F   Forward
0 Other Options          H   Help

NEXT COMMAND:
```

```
Subject Request: S=MULTICULTURALISM                              DWIL
WILSON RECORD      1 of 29 Entries Found                    View Record
VVVVVVVVVVVVVVVVVVVVVVVVVVVVVVVVVVVVVVVVVVVVVVVVVVVVVVVVVVVVVVVVVVVVVVVVV

AUTHORS:            Kondracke, Morton

ARTICLE TITLE:      Blenders

SOURCE/DATE:        The New Republic   207:50  Sep 21 '92

SPECIAL FEATURES:   il.

SUBJECT DESCRIPTORS:
                    Population forecasting
                    Immigrants
                    Interacial marriage
                    Multiculturalism

VVVVVVVVVVVVVVVVVVVVVVVVVVVVVVVVVVVVVVVVVVVVVVVVVVVVVVVVVVVVVVVVVVVVVVVVV
COMMANDS:           HO   Holdings      H   Help
                    N    Next Record
0 Other Options     I    Index

Held by library  type HO for holdings information
NEXT COMMAND:
```

There is no "see" reference. DWIL's first article descriptors "Population Forecasting," "Immigrants," "Interracial Marriage" and "Multiculturalism" do not compliment DPACs subject headings. DWIL does not follow Library of Congress guidelines. The inconsistency between databases frustrates many users and decreases their chances of locating relevant data.

A look at two additional searches illustrates the confusion many patrons encounter when searching automated indexes.

```
ProQuest                CD-ROM Retrieval              Version 4
Periodical Abstracts-Research II Jan 1991-Jan 1993  F1=Help F2=Command


     multiculturalism


     Press _____|  to view records

                        Press _____| to view a list of
                        titles or F7 to view full
                        records retrieved by your search



  Num              Search                          Hits

  #2               multiculturalism                 718



     Press TAB to access previous results

Type your search and press _____|



ProQuest                CD-ROM Retrieval              Version 4
Periodical Abstracts Research II Jan 1991-Jan 1993  F1=Help  F2=Command



                     Item 1 of 718

New York Times  Jan 10, 1993  Sec. 4A  p. 18    Press _____| to view
                                                full records

Stanford reflects campus diversity
New York Times  Jan 10, 1993  Sec. 4A  p. 21    Press F9 to mark items
                                                for printing or saving
                                                to a disk.

Walcott blasts 'Ethnic Cleansing'. in Europe
Jet  Dec 28, 1992   p. 24
                                                Press F4 to print/
                                                save to a disk.

Under 'Rainbow' a War: When Politics, Moral
New York Times  Dec 27, 1992  Sec. A, p. 34
```

Follow the Star
Times Educational Supplement   Dec 25, 1992 p   Press F7 to view Library
                                                      Holdings Information.

All in a Year's Work-Beyond Walls and Wars:
Village Voice   Dec 22, 1992 p. 64

Item Availability: Unknown

        to move. Press _____| to display full record.   ESC=go back

    Follow The Star
    Times Educational supplement   Dec 25, 1992 p   Press F7 to view
                                                    Library holdings
                                                    Information
    All in a Year's Work-Beyond Walls and Wars
    Village Voice Dec 22, 1992   p. 64
    Item Availability: Unknown

        to move. Press _____| to display full record ESC=go back

Access No: 02153290   ProQuest Periodical Abstracts
Title: St. John's clings to the classics
Journal: New York Times (NYT) ISSN: 0362-4331
                  Date: Jan 10, 1993 Sec: A p: 18 Col: 3
                  Type: News   Length: Medium   Illus: Illustration

Companies: St. John's College-Annapolis MD

Subjects: Multiculturalism & pluralism; Series & Special
                  reports; Literature; Curricula; Colleges &
                  Universities; Education reform

Abstract: Although colleges across the nation are abandoning
    the Western canon and looking more to multicultural education,
    St. John's College of Annapolis MD is sticking true to its curriculum
    centering on the works of Homer, Plato, Aristotle, Machiavelli,
    Nietzsche and others.

ProQuest   CD-ROM Retrieval   Version 4.0
Newspaper Abstracts Ondisc Jan 1992-Jan 1993   F1=Help F2=Command

    multiculturalism

        Press _____| to view records

                    Press _____| to view a list of
                    titles or F7 to view full
                    records retrieved by your search.

        Num   Search   Hits

        #1   multiculturalism   206

            Press TAB to access previous results

Type your search and press _____|

ProQuest   CD-ROM Retrieval   Version 4.0
Newspaper Abstracts Ondisc   Jan 1992-Jan 1993   F1=Help   F2=Command

Item 1 of 206

Los Angeles Times   Jan 31, 1993   Sec. M   p. 5
Summer Festivals enliven Sydney
Christian Science Monitor   Jan 29, 1993   p. 11
Its Southern pride, battered and fried
Atlanta Constitution   Jan 29, 1993   Sec. G   p. 1
Hunter gets curriculum covering many cultures
New York Times   Jan 28, 1993   Sec. B   p. 3
Honor great works on their own terms
Chicago Tribune   Jan 28, 1993   Sec. 1   p. 18

In tribal solitude
New York Times   Jan 26, 1993   Sec. A   p. 23

        to move. Press _____| to display full record.   ESC=Go back

Chicago Tribune   Jan. 28, 1993   Sec. 1   p. 18

In Tribal solitude
New York Times   Jan. 26, 1993   Sec. A   p. 23

        to move. Press _____| to display full record   ESC=Go back

Access No.:   02184389 ProQuest - Newspaper Abstracts
Title: Put 'rainbow' back in the closet
Authors: McMillan, Susan Carpenter
Source: Los Angeles Times (LAT)   ISSN: 0458-3035
                     Date: Jan 31, 1993   Sec: M   p: 5   Col: 5
                     Type: Commentary   Length: Medium
Companies: Unified School District-Los Angeles CA
Subjects: Curricula; Homosexuality; Multiculturalism &
                     pluralism

Abstract: Susan Carpenter McMillan criticizes the Los
Angeles Unified School District for rumors that it will consider
adopting the 'Children of the Rainbow' multicultural curriculum,
which mandates the teaching of homosexuality as a normal lifestyle.

The Newspaper index search resulted in 206 hits and the Periodicals index search resulted in 718 hits. The first article in each of the databases concerns the multicultural curriculum. One focuses on post secondary institutions and the other is about the curriculum in secondary schools. The remaining articles are incompatible incorporating a wide range of subjects. They require researchers to spend an exorbitant amount of time examining titles in the hope of finding appropriate material. For many reference librarians, working in the electronic environment, students wading through hundreds of articles in hope of finding pertinent material is a familiar sight. Boolean connectors may be used to combine search terms and specify searches, but this method frequently increases search results exponentially; for most researchers this once again results in sorting through numerous articles. The disparity of search results continues to increase as the patron transfers to different databases. Until information retrieval systems adopt universally recognized cataloging rules many computerized searches will remain sloppy and useless.

In summary, unlike the students described in this essay many researchers do not ask for assistance. Many users experience the changes taking place in libraries as barriers to finding the information they seek. Developers of information retrieval systems can reverse this view of their product by adopting comprehensive cataloging standards while remaining sensitive to user needs. Catalogers should also be aware of the effect controversy surrounding a subject has on the way they perform their job and arrange data sensitively.

Librarians have the power to prepare individuals to locate information in the emerging electronic environment. They must be empathetic to the individuals they assist. Information Science curriculums should address this issue in courses and librarians should be trained to instruct users in database searching and the use of command language. This will prepare them to teach information management in credit bearing classes, during library orientations, and on-site in reference areas. These steps combined with the implementation of cataloging standards can make the library attractive to all researchers and reduce the complexity of locating information on controversial and other topics.

REFERENCES

D'Souza, D. (1991). Multiculturalism 101. *Policy Review*, 56, 22-30.

Gambino, R. (1992). From the one many: The multiculturalist threat. *Current*, 347, 35-39.

Holderness, M. (1992). Time to shelve the library? (Electronic future for information. *New Scientist, 136*, 22-23.

Kessler-Harris, A. (1992). Multiculturalism can strengthen, not undermine, a common culture. *The Chronicle of Higher Education*, b3-b7.

Robinson, O. H. (1986). College libraries as aids to instruction: Rochester University library–administration and use. In L. L. Hardesty, J. P. Schmitt & J. M. Tucker (Eds.), *User instruction in academic libraries* (pp. 17-35). Metuchen, NJ: The Scarecrow Press, Inc.

Schlesinger, A. M. Jr. (1991) Writing, and rewriting, history. *The New Leader, 74*, 12-14.

Smoler, F. (1992). What should we teach our children about American history? *American Heritage, 43*, 45-52.

Wong, F. F. (1991). Diversity and community. *Change, 23*, 48-54.

Preparing Librarians
for the Twenty-First Century–
Assuring That They Will Measure Up

W. David Penniman

SUMMARY. Schools of library/information science need to be restructured. One model would be to offer courses (and a Bachelor's degree) that would emphasize methods. Further education, with an emphasis on administration and scholarship, would be the place for graduate degrees. The vulnerabilities of schools of library/information studies are listed. Finally, an evaluation of these schools is outlined. *[Single or multiple copies of this article are available from The Haworth Document Delivery Service: 1-800-342-9678, 9:00 a.m. - 5:00 p.m. (EST).]*

KEYWORDS. Library/information science curricula, library/information science education-accreditation, library/information services professions

I do not intend to focus on diversity *per se* though I do have something to say about that. Instead, I want to focus on change in general and set the framework for the remainder of the day. Today more than ever, we face the challenge of ensuring the relevance of our educational systems for preparation of tomorrow's professionals. This is a statement not limited to library and information sci-

Dr. W. David Penniman is President of the Council on Library Resources, Washington, DC.

[Haworth co-indexing entry note]: "Preparing Librarians for the Twenty-First Century–Assuring That They Will Measure Up." Penniman, W. David. Co-published simultaneously in *Public & Access Services Quarterly* (The Haworth Press, Inc.) Vol. 1, No. 3, 1995, pp. 85-95; and: *Mapping Curricular Reform in Library/Information Studies Education: The American Mosaic* (ed: Virgil L. P. Blake) The Haworth Press, Inc., 1995, pp. 85-95. Single or multiple copies of this article are available from The Haworth Document Delivery Service [1-800-342-9678, 9:00 a.m. - 5:00 p.m. (EST)].

ence education, but also applies to programs throughout our universities and colleges. The Workforce 2000 report[1] as well as other projections indicate the radical changes in our work forces to come. Our current educational systems and their associated accreditation may be neither sufficient (nor even necessary) to assure the survival of a particular school or program. Furthermore, is mere survival enough or is it only a temporary assurance?

In a report[2] issued well before the most recent announcements of UCLA and UC Berkley, the American Library Association (ALA) was advised not to intervene in local decisions on college and university campuses to close specific library schools. Instead, the ALA was told that:

> (it) should be concerned about the educational needs of our profession not because some of our accredited schools are closing, but because the information age is forcing changes which are affecting job content and staffing needs of agencies in the information society.

The report continued that if ALA were to take action, it would be best aimed at the future of libraries and information services and the human and intellectual resources that will be needed to serve the profession in the future.

It may not be surprising, then, to find that the Council on Library Resources has selected as one of its program areas that of HUMAN RESOURCES FOR INFORMATION SERVICES, with a major focus on the end-to-end process of attracting, developing, and educating on a continuing basis the talent necessary for the profession. The program, in addition, is concerned with leadership development, mentoring, and a wide range of issues in attracting sufficient diversity within the profession.

Today, however, I am not here to focus on the Council's programs, though they are related to the issues of concern. Today, I am here to talk about ways we have approached the problems of educating professionals for our field. I intend to present my talk in two parts.

The first part will challenge your thinking, I believe, regarding library school status and structure. It should raise some concern about leadership and readiness to change. You may find the first part a little difficult. I certainly did in putting it together. I want to try to refute the cynical view that leadership in our time is the quality of telling people what they want to hear. The idea has most recently been expressed in the best selling book, *Rising Sun,*[3] about United States industry and Japanese competition.

The second part of my talk looks at library schools and librarians in terms of what measures might be used to evaluate library schools, as well as what librarianship should and should not be. I'll mention some projects that the Council has helped in this area.

So, now to the first part of this presentation.

The library world of the future cannot now be surveyed, it is true, but certain tendencies clearly apparent today afford clues to the development of the next few decades. The tendencies contain an element of forecast that predicts "there will have to come a change in emphasis in library education."

It may be necessary always for thoroughly prepared librarians to become familiar in some measure with the entire range of the present discipline; but as they fit themselves for the larger aspects of work, this will sink into the position of a nucleus, essential but relatively small.

The present thesis is not that library school curricula . . . should be reshaped to meet a new order of library service which is only in the early stages of its development, but that whatever the accrediting body (Committee on Accreditation) urges or decrees in the next few years should be such as to key in with the eventual system of education so far as this can be discerned now. In other words, prepare for change.

Briefly . . . it seems reasonable to picture a structure ranging from fundamental training classes within libraries themselves to graduate programs that consist of a coordinated series of courses carefully defined and grouped in curricula appropriate to the respective aims of the various institutions by which they may be offered.

With this is assumed a certifying agency, so situated as to view the entire field of library service and to measure the qualifications of professionals in light of the requirements of the service. The agency should automatically relieve library schools of the accrediting function now settled on them.

The acceptance of distinctions separating clerical and professional library service is, of course, understood. But, let's be clear about what is now needed. Instruction for preparation in professional services should begin with:

1. Undergraduate education for the lower grades of library professionals based on knowledge of method.
2. Graduate study should prepare individuals for scholarly and administrative work, based on knowledge of subjects and of sources.

This arrangement would suggest that the degree of Bachelor of Science in Library Science be awarded to students who took certain prescribed courses as part of their undergraduate programs; that a Master of Library Science to students who, after having taken certain prerequisites as undergraduates, took certain prescribed courses and certain groupings of elected courses and prepared thesis, their work extending over a year of graduate study; and that a Doctor of Library Science, or Ph.D., to students who, after the appropriate undergraduate prerequisites, prepared doctor's theses, and spent three years on a program of study combining prescribed courses, elective courses in library school and other departments.

The plan proposed would ultimately result in the breaking out of the traditional library school curriculum, as it now exists. From the standpoint of the library schools now requiring a bachelor's degree for admission, the plan would seem like a lowering of standards. It provides for three years academic work and one year of professional study for every person having professional status, and for one or two or three years of graduate work with appropriate degrees for all persons who wished to qualify for more scholarly or responsible positions. I believe that, with the reorganizing of curricula on a time saving basis, and with the incentive of a certification scheme, the plan would result in a material improvement in calibre of our professional personnel, to say nothing of the fact that individuals would enjoy far greater chance to develop their specific abilities, and, therefore, would be fitted to provide superior service.

As things stand in library schools today, they are putting competent, mature, and broadly educated men and women through courses which often seem to be semi-clerical and predominately concerned with method. If men and women of ability are to be drawn into the profession, it is essential that they are not led to think that library education is mainly technique. Some technique must be kept, but it should not occupy so large a place, as it has to date.

Librarians in increasing numbers are concerned about the prestige which academic degrees confer, yet often do not understand that the degrees available don't confer much prestige. In summary, persons who wish professional status should have four years of study leading to a Bachelor's degree. Three of these years would be general academic and one year library school subjects. Those who wished to go on could secure a Master's degree and not only fit themselves for higher grades of service, but assure themselves the academic recognition which present library degrees cannot command.

Now, before I go to the second part of my talk, let me say that what I have presented up to this point was written for me and for you seven decades ago by Ernest J. Reece,[4] Principal of the Library School of the New York Public Library. His recommendations were published by the ALA in 1924 as a pamphlet titled "Some Possible Developments in Library Education." His points seem equally relevant today. What I gleaned from his words were:

1. The future can't be predicted, but trends can be seen and we must prepare to change.
2. There will be a need for increasing specialization in our field.
3. Our degree programs need restructuring, and the first professional degree should be granted at the undergraduate level. Advanced degrees should be conferred, but consistent with broader institutional aims and professional requirements.
4. A certifying agency should be created that relieves the schools of that function. Certifying is for individuals in this context.
5. Current schools put bright, competent, mature students through routine technique-oriented courses. This must cease if schools are to attract individuals of high calibre.
6. And finally, the prestige of the degree is diminished. A new structure is needed.

Many of those same points have been made by others more recently in various ways. In 1979, L. Heilprin delivered a presentation at the Maryland Library Association, and subsequently, it was published twice in the *Journal of the American Society for Informa-*

tion Science. In 1980 and ten years later that piece titled "The Library Community at a Technological and Philosophical Crosswords: Necessary and Sufficient Conditions for Survival"[5] called for continual educational renewal or else the profession would be replaced by faster adapting communities. C. McClure and C. Hart wrote a piece[6] calling for specialization in library/information science education (shades of the seventy year old pamphlet just reviewed). A. Woodsworth and J. Lester also published an article[7] on the educational imperatives of the future research library that defined the set of competencies necessary to run the future research library. And just recently J. Campbell has published an article in *American Libraries* titled "Choosing to Have a Future"[8] that calls for accrediting agencies to bless and even encourage new directions and experiments in library education. He tells librarians to show courageous self confidence, and undertake large-scale changes. He points out that no one can precisely predict or completely control the outcome of change–we can only initiate it.

But a recent meeting[9] of over a dozen library school deans (with support from the CLR) concluded that there were many reasons why library schools may be left out of the picture when change does occur. Some of those reasons included:

- subcritical size
- lack of visibility
- isolation and defensiveness
- parochial thinking
- lack of understanding of the intellectual core, complexity and substance of the field
- professional needs that go beyond the current scope of our professional societies
- lack of a tradition of teamwork
- shortage of visionary leadership
- low standards and expectations
- lack of a continuous, cumulative research base
- need for user-centered research rather than focus on history and analysis

The same group concluded that there were strong reasons for information and library science schools to be in the picture. These included:

- The true core of this profession is unique, and needs to influence the shape of information services to come.
- Our profession can bring a focus on intellectual access and a user-centered approach to systems and services.
- Demand for information professionals will grow.

How can we tell if our schools are doing the job? Let me suggest some specific measures:

1. Does the school's vision and mission mesh with its parent institutions direction?
2. Does the school break even financially, or does it require subsidy (beyond normal support of its parent institution) to exist?
3. Does it strengthen or weaken the financial condition of the parent institution?
4. Are enrollments growing, shrinking, or plateaued? Have they been capped for economic reasons?
5. Are student qualifications higher or lower than in the past?
6. Are their qualifications above or below the median of other schools on campus?
7. Do students and faculty represent the multiethnic and multicultural cross section of our nation and of library users?
8. Are the faculty engaged in research that is acknowledged by academicians in other related fields as credible?
   Corollary: Are the faculty engaged in interdisciplinary work; and are they sought out for such work?
9. Are library faculty working with libraries and librarians on collaborative projects?
10. Do students leave the school satisfied?
11. Are they satisfied five or ten years later with what the school sold them?
12. Are the graduates of the program commanding significant jobs in their chosen specialty? (Significance can be measured in terms of responsibility, status of hiring institution, salary,

or whatever means you choose, but it can and should be tracked.)

13. Are the more experienced graduates influencing the evolution of our societies' information systems? Are they providing leadership?

I believe, as do the deans who met recently at an ASIS (American Society for Information Science) mid-year meeting, that librarians can shape our emerging information environment in ways seldom available to them in the past. In the past, librarians have been required to take information as packaged, and store it for subsequent use by their clients. In order to do this efficiently, librarians have developed strong skills in information selection and organization. These skills can serve libraries well in playing a major role further upstream in the information production process than they have been allowed to participate in to date. Librarians' knowledge of user needs and information seeking characteristics makes them a very desirable partner in the new electronic world. But, librarians must not wait to be asked to play in this arena. Librarians must find an aggressive role to play, and do it. Librarians must be the kind of partners other key players will actively seek, and library schools must encourage their students to play an active role.

The forces on the profession are profound. While technology plays a major role in the change process, so will financial and social forces. Because the profession has been tied inextricably to the library as an institution, the changes in the library itself will affect the profession as the profession influences the library. As each changes, the other must change to keep pace. But, librarianship goes far beyond the walls of the library, and it will do so even more as the focus shifts more dramatically to access (rather than ownership). As this occurs, it will become even clearer what the profession is and is not.

Librarianship is not a "professional" safe haven for disenchanted intellectuals who want to escape the politics of organizations and people for the peacefulness of books.

Librarianship is not a profession with little or no knowledge of technology, management theory and practice, economic and financial principles, and organizational development is required or appears in educational preparation.

Librarianship is not an "entitled profession" where funding for activities will be automatic because their implicit good is recognized by those controlling the resources.

Librarianship is not a homogeneous profession lacking sufficient diversity to respond adequately to the changing user audiences of the institutions they will serve.

And librarianship is not a profession that serves first and foremost the needs of an institution called the library when that institution is defined by the walls of a building that accumulates and houses books and other information "assets."

Librarianship is a leading profession (in every sense of the word) for the twenty-first century. Librarianship is at the forefront in service, leadership, innovation, and recruitment and development of its people. It should promote the design of information systems that require little or no learning time for effective use. It should take responsibility for information policy development, information technology application, and information research.

Librarians should experiment with new forms of organizational structure and staffing within libraries, and should recognize and support the concept of the library without walls, as well as the capacity of library services to be provided in a variety of settings. The profession must strengthen its degree-granting programs, and attract and retain creative and innovative people of great diversity. It must incorporate different competencies/professions and address the importance of continuing professional education. This is what it can and should do. What values set librarianship apart from other professions? Librarians value privacy, confidentiality, intellectual freedom, users' ability to independently find information, awareness of the role of the librarian in the community, literacy, and continuing professional education.

I have just summarized for you the product of a Council project involving the vision and values of librarianship in the twenty-first century.[10]

And that brings me at last to my vision of the future for the institution we call the library. I look to a future where libraries continue to play a vital societal role. What do I believe the library of tomorrow will look like? Will it be accessed from my briefcase like the emerging personal assistants with telecommunication links and up/downloading capabilities that begin to fulfill the information industry's dream of "information anywhere, anytime?"

Will it be a place–a building (of suitably stunning architecture) where people may go? Or will it be in our homes? Most people have television sets–could this be where people "go" in the future for their "library" information?

All of these may be parts of the library of tomorrow. I prefer, however, to describe the library of tomorrow by describing the users of tomorrow. Our users must become independent problem solvers who know how to use information resources to address the challenges that face them (which include the challenges of educating and entertaining themselves), and that idea will shape the library of the future in ways we may not even be able to imagine today. But, we must be sure that our library and information science schools are preparing professionals who will help those users of the future. For our schools to do that they must not only survive, they must thrive.

That must be the role of the accrediting process, that is, to assure that our schools have built in the necessary mechanisms for continuous evolution. As Jerry Campbell has said, "We can not predict change–we can only initiate it." It is time, past time, for our schools to evolve–and the accrediting process must play a significant role in driving this evolution. Otherwise, why have such a process? Decades from now we must see more progress than Reece would see if he were here today.

REFERENCES

1. William Johnson and Arnold Packer, *Workforce 2000* (Washington, D.C.: U.S. Department of Labor, 1987).

2. Russell Shank, Pat Molholt, Patricia H. Mautino, Marion Paris and William F. Summers, "ALA Special Committee on Library Closings Report," (Chicago: American Library Association) June 15, 1991. Photocopy.

3. Michael Crichton; *Rising Sun* (New York: Ballantine Books, 1992).

4. Ernest J. Reece, *Some Possible Developments in Library Education* (Chicago: American Library Association, 1924).

5. Laurence B. Heilprin, "The Library Community at a Technological and Philosophical Crossroads: Necessary and Sufficient Conditions for Survival," *Journal of the American Society for information Science,* 31, 6 (November, 1980), p. 389-395.

6. Charles R. McClure and Carol A. Hart, "Specialization in Library information Science Education: Issues, Scenarios, and the Need for Action." Paper presented at the meeting, Conference on Specialization in Library/Information Science Education, Ann Arbor, Michigan, November 6-8, 1991.

7. Anne Woodsworth and June Lester, "Educational Imperatives of the Future Research Library: A Symposium," *The Journal of Academic Librarianship,* 17, (September, 1991), p. 204-209.

8. Jerry D. Campbell, "Choosing To Have A Future," *American Libraries,* 24, 6 (June, 1993), p. 560-566.

9. Daniel E. Atkins, "The Changing Curriculum and Research for the Electronic Library." Paper presented at the meeting, Library of Congress Network Advisory Committee, June 13-15, 1993.

10. Susan K. Martin, "Librarians on a Tightrope: Getting from Here to There and Loosening Up in the Process." *After the Electronic Revolution, Will You Be the First to Go?* Proceedings of the 1992 Association for Library Collections and Technical Services, Presidents Program, American Library Association Annual Conference, San Francisco, California, June 29, 1992. Edited by Arnold Hirshon (Chicago: American Library Association, 1993).

Moving Beyond Cliche:
Cultural Diversity and the Curriculum
in Library and Information Studies

William C. Welburn

SUMMARY. There are four basic issues to be resolved in any consideration of cultural diversity and library/information science education. An effective response to curriculum reform mandates the development of specific responses to each of these. *[Single or multiple copies of this article are available from The Haworth Document Delivery Service: 1-800-342-9678, 9:00 a.m. - 5:00 p.m. (EST).]*

KEYWORDS. Multiculturalism in library/information science education, curriculum reform-basic issues, goals of curriculum reform in library/information science education

In the introduction to her new book, *As Various as Their Land: the Everyday Lives of Eighteenth Century Americans*, Stephanie Grauman Wolf characterized the reconstruction of the Colonial American mosaic in the following way:

> The center stage of history has always been occupied by great events . . . and the great men who acted in them. But for every Cotton Mather, Samuel Adams, Benjamin Franklin, or George

---

William C. Welburn is Dean of the Graduate College, The University of Iowa, Iowa City, IA.

[Haworth co-indexing entry note]: "Moving Beyond Cliche: Cultural Diversity and the Curriculum in Library and Information Studies." Welburn, William C. Co-published simultaneously in *Public & Access Services Quarterly* (The Haworth Press, Inc.) Vol. 1, No. 3, 1995, pp. 97-100; and: *Mapping Curricular Reform in Library/Information Studies Education: The American Mosaic* (ed: Virgil L. P. Blake) The Haworth Press, Inc., 1995, pp. 97-100. Single or multiple copies of this article are available from The Haworth Document Delivery Service [1-800-342-9678, 9:00 a.m. - 5:00 p.m. (EST)].

Washington there were hundreds of assemblymen, clergymen, and judges; thousands of people who made up mobs, polls, and armies; and tens of thousands of farmers, artisans, laborers, women, children, servants, and slaves. The daily lives of all of these people . . . formed the real web of the eighteenth century, creating the setting and conditions for history's dramatic changes, as well as responding to those changes.[1]

It is of central importance in our discussions of multiculturalism at the end of the twentieth century that we view the American mosaic in it's historical context; that the shaping of American values and cultures over the centuries has been done by a diversity of people held together by a common history. And it is incumbent that educators are challenged to do what Michael Dorris recently suggested, to move "beyond cliche, beyond politics"[2] and accept multiculturalism as essential to curricular reform.

Elsewhere I have proposed that when library and information science programs, and for that matter other professional education programs, consider cultural diversity and curricular reform, that we are challenged only with two major factors: to understand and teach about technologies and to understand and teach about people. While library and information studies educators have been effective in articulating a technological agenda,[3] we have done this without a parallel discussion on people who, to paraphrase Stephanie Grauman Wolf, form the real web of our society.

I would like to recommend four important elements to curricular reform in library and information studies that take cultural diversity into consideration. However, I wish to preface these points by endorsing the idea that librarianship is a *mediating* profession. As a mediating profession we are at the center of a dynamic interplay between people and information. It is imperative that we recognize the role of culture in each of the three elements that compose this relationship: the cultural contexts of *information, its origins and uses,* of *information seekers,* and of *information mediators* or *providers*. All three elements ought to have a major impact on how we teach students entering librarianship and related information professions.

Based on this model, to date I have identified four issues that are appropriate for a discussion of the American Mosaic and its demands upon curriculum in library and information studies. First, we must embark on a program of faculty development in library and information studies programs that focuses on the interrelationships between people and information, specifically recognizing the central role of culture and cultural diversity. There is a paucity of scholarship on racial/ethnic or multicultural perspectives on library and information science. This can be contrasted with law, where a large albeit controversial body of literature has emerged in critical legal studies, particularly in the areas of race and feminist theory. If we are to teach cultural diversity inside our curriculum, we will need more faculty who are actively engaged in research and scholarship in this area.

Second, we must focus our attention on pedagogical approaches to teaching *majority* students in schools of library and information studies. ALISE data confirm that there are few schools in the United States where students of color are in the majority. In an article on multiculturalism and teaching students in family therapy, Rona Preli and Janine Bernard argued for the integration of two contradictory assumptions: that the majority culture represents a homogeneous group and that the entire population of the United States consists of individual ethnic and cultural identities. They believe, and I concur, that while it is essential for majority students in our schools to understand multiculturalism within the European American population, there is also an important difference between European American ethnic identity and ethnic populations of color.[4] In other words, understanding individual student's own ethnicity becomes a framework for communicating and working across cultures. It has the effect of *leveling the playing field.*

Third, recognition of cultural diversity as an important ingredient in the makeup of the student body can enhance the quality of the educational experience within our programs in library and information science. We should not engage in an effort to increase the numbers of students of color in our programs solely for the purpose of recruiting more racial and ethnic minorities into the profession. Rather, improving the quality of educational experience is enough justification for diversity regardless of fluctuation in demand from the field. There are examples of other academic programs in my university that have successfully related a sustained or increased quality in educational programming with a broader diversity among students.

Finally, we must seek to broaden the educational backgrounds and experiences of the students we admit to our programs. We continually argue for the need to recruit more students with science backgrounds and excellent quantitative analytical skills. We should add to our requirements academic training in race and ethnicity, gender, intercultural communication, poverty, or other forms of social and cultural understanding.

These four issues, when combined with our reconstructed understanding of America's history and culture, can serve as a blueprint for curricular change in library and information science in the 1990s.

NOTES

1. Stephanie Grauman Wolf. *As Various as Their Land: the Everyday Lives of Eighteenth-Century Americans.* New York: Harper-Collins, 1993. p. 11.

2. Michael Dorris, "Beyond Cliche, Beyond Politics: Multiculturalism and the Fact of America." *Georgia Review* 46 (Fall 1992): 407-17.

3. In this paper, technology refers to the tasks performed within an organization in the broadest sense of the word, including the provision, utilization and management of information for use by clientele.

4. Rona Preli and Janine M. Bernard, "Making Multiculturalism Relevant for Majority Culture Graduate Students," *Journal of Marital and Family Therapy* 19 (January 1993): p. 5-16.

Multicultural Approach
for Curriculum Development
in the Library and Information Sciences:
Where Are We Going?

Ana N. Arzu

SUMMARY. A major obstacle to attracting students from cultural/ ethnic/linguistic minorities is the professional stereotype. Removing this is a first step in increasing minority representation in the profession. A second step would require that schools of library/information science identify people-oriented individuals and actively recruit them. With these preliminary steps and minor adjustments to the current curriculum, library/information science education can make strides in diversity. *[Single or multiple copies of this article are available from The Haworth Document Delivery Service: 1-800-342-9678, 9:00 a.m. - 5:00 p.m. (EST).]*

KEYWORDS. Perception of library/information services, pre-requisites for the library/information science curriculum, recruiting among minority populations

Finally, after several hundred years of suffering at each others hands just because we've been under the misconception that one

---

Ana N. Arzu is Law Librarian at the Office of the Queens County District Attorney, Borough of Queens, Kew Gardens, NY.

[Haworth co-indexing entry note]: "Multicultural Approach for Curriculum Development in the Library and Information Sciences: Where Are We Going?" Arzu, Ana N. Co-published simultaneously in *Public & Access Services Quarterly* (The Haworth Press, Inc.) Vol. 1, No. 3, 1995, pp. 101-104; and: *Mapping Curricular Reform in Library/Information Studies Education: The American Mosaic* (ed: Virgil L. P. Blake) The Haworth Press, Inc., 1995, pp. 101-104. Single or multiple copies of this article are available from The Haworth Document Delivery Service [1-800-342-9678, 9:00 a.m. - 5:00 p.m. (EST)].

race is superior to another, or one sex is superior to the other or one school of thought or way of thinking is superior than any other, we are awakened by the alarm clock of multiculturalism. Judging from the newspaper headlines and other articles that document our history, multiculturalism is not only a word but it is an absolute reality. It is something that must be. This is proof that we're finally willing to accept the irrefutable fact that all of us, on this planet, have evolved in different cultures, different directions, and have each with our own virtues made valuable contributions to this civilization.

Where do we, librarians, storers and disseminators of information who recognize the power and influence of knowledge fit in? I will begin with a word "multiculturalism" and in terms of this conference "multicultural curriculum reform." I am delighted to meet with you today in this American Mosaic in the hope of identifying our responsibility as professionals in library and information science. I will be addressing three issues: the multicultural aspect of curriculum reform, the underlying theme of professionalism in adjusting to the rapid changes that must be faced by our profession, and drawing on my ten years of involvement in law library management I would like to share my personal view on how the curriculum can be developed.

Somewhere in the corridors of my mind I keep hoping that this reform not turn out to be like other reforms in the past. In the past, curriculum reform, as I have known it, has taken the shape of making things less challenging. Personally, I feel that reforming a curriculum to accommodate minorities by means of making the curriculum less academically challenging is nothing short of insulting. I sincerely hope this is not what we are attempting here. I feel that our curriculum reform should begin at the most fundamental level–us. I think we should begin by being proud of our profession and behave accordingly so as to attract people from all walks of life.

Earlier this year I participated in career day at a high school.[1] I was part of a panel of role models for careers in the legal profession. I was amazed that as brilliant as these particular children were, they had no idea that my profession existed. I began by asking them what they thought I did. Their comments were as follows: you have a boring job, it must be relaxing, you sit down a lot and take care of books, you have to dress a certain way, only white people get those jobs, how did you get yours? The comment that angered me the most was "you have to have a law degree to be a Law Librarian." They were silenced and listened more intently when I began explaining what I actually do.

They were very impressed to learn about the tremendous diverseness of my work: As a Law Librarian I am expected to know what is inside the lawbooks, studying is therefore a large part of my job. I also have to know how the law is organized, published and be able to train my end users in finding the law. Public relations is a large part of my job. I have to know what publications are out there and select the preferred ones for my end users. Budgeting and shopping are part of my job; I buy publications and library supplies from a budget I am expected to balance. Computer skills also are part of my job; I sit on the Automation Think Tank together with MIS, I designed an on-line catalog to go on our wide area network and, I am currently working on an automated brief bank for our legal briefs that will also go on the wide area network. I am also expected to be a teacher in my role as a librarian: I give two annual legal research training lectures to all new incoming Assistant District Attorneys. I knew I had reached the students when their hands went up. They either had to go to the bathroom or they had questions–and they had questions! The first question was "What school do you recommend we go to prepare us for a job like yours?" There was silence and I experienced one of those rare moments when I had nothing to say. I gave them the names of various schools, but my tone of voice let them know that school alone is not the answer. The qualities I have that permit me to function as a Law Librarian for the District Attorney were not learned in Library School. I learned primarily from working with others, continuing on my own to keep abreast of current literature on library and information science, and by always striving to be very attentive to the needs of my library users.

In my view, curriculum development in all areas of knowledge, including library and information science, should be primarily a human effort enabling people of all cultures and genders to best meet the expectations of society for the professions involved, while at the same time giving due recognition to the diversity among people of our world. If diversity in the cultural mosaic is to be successful, then more emphasis must be placed on providing a curriculum that emphasizes development of people skills and the ability to cope with the real world of the work place. Too many people are confused about what librarians really do, and I believe we are partly responsible for this misconception because we seldom discuss what we do with people outside of our circles. It is important that we emerge from our xenophobic state and reach out into society. Doing this will dispel the librarian myths that keep society from appreciating our true value and keep our salaries behind the times (which is another paper). It will also send the message that this is not an elitist, white dominated, law-degree profession but rather a profession that is welcoming to people from all walks of life. But before we reform anything lets come to grips with this reality: our whole world is undergoing constant and rapid change. This change must be taken into account by our profession if it is to be viable.

MLS curriculum is failing to come to terms with change and to recognize the evolving merger of librarians and the managers of information. The library is no longer a static organized compilation of books. The library of today is so active and so alive it's almost organic. It's shape, style and function has undergone complete metamorphosis. It is imperative that the designers of the MLS curriculum reassess what librarians are actually doing in their place of work and then redefine the skills needed to shape and preserve the profession. The creators of the curriculum have to admit that the place of libraries has changed. We need a curriculum that produces librarians who believe they are more than just custodians of books.

NOTE

1. Boys and Girls High School, Brooklyn.

Find 'Em or Grow Your Own:
Recruitment and Retention of Minorities
in the Library Profession

Karen Thorburn

SUMMARY. Given the small number of library/information service professionals from minority groups the profession can not afford to fail to make recruiting from cultural/ethnic/linguistic minorities a priority. This will require innovative recruiting tactics on the part of current professionals to guide para-professionals, non-professionals and volunteers to entering this profession. It will require some degree of flexibility on the part of schools of library/information science to meet the needs of these students. Employers too will have to make it possible for current staff who desire it to complete their professional education. Administrators have a role in creating staffing patterns to foster further education. *[Single or multiple copies of this article are available from The Haworth Document Delivery Service: 1-800-342-9678, 9:00 a.m. - 5:00 p.m. (EST).]*

KEYWORDS. Minority representation in library/information service, innovative recruiting, role of library/information science education in educating minorities, role of employing libraries/information centers, role of administrators in recruiting and retaining

While the percentage of minorities in the general population has shown a steady increase, and now stands at more than 20%, less

---

Karen Thorburn is Director of the Plainfield Public Library, Plainfield, NJ.

[Haworth co-indexing entry note]: "Find 'Em or Grow Your Own: Recruitment and Retention of Minorities in the Library Profession." Thorburn, Karen. Co-published simultaneously in *Public & Access Services Quarterly* (The Haworth Press, Inc.) Vol. 1, No. 3, 1995, pp. 105-115; and: *Mapping Curricular Reform in Library/Information Studies Education: The American Mosaic* (ed: Virgil L. P. Blake) The Haworth Press, Inc., 1995, pp. 105-115. Single or multiple copies of this article are available from The Haworth Document Delivery Service [1-800-342-9678, 9:00 a.m. - 5:00 p.m. (EST)].

than 11.5% of the librarians are minorities. This is significant in that the percentage actually decreased from 11.8% between 1980 and 1985. By the year 2000 the percentage of minorities in the general population will have increased to almost one third. The question is, will minority representation in our profession keep pace?

In 1989 minorities made up only 8% of those receiving Masters degrees in Library Science. The under representation of African-Americans simply reflects the general societal problem of racial inequality. Librarianship is no worse than, and in most cases better than, most professions–such as Law, Physics, Medicine, etc. While minorities are less under-represented in this than in the general professional population, we as librarians should be in the forefront of the move toward racial equity in our staffs.

As librarians we have an obligation to answer the challenge of minority recruitment and retention, consciously setting aside a certain portion of our recruitment resources and efforts to bring minorities into the profession. The major corporations are making inroads into the problem by designating diversity officers, and by hiring specific numbers of minorities in order to meet their corporate goals. But while AT&T can decide to hire twelve minority Senior Vice Presidents and then go out and do it, libraries must work within the systems, which for too long have only perpetuated the inequities of the past. Libraries must bear an even greater responsibility, shared perhaps only by Higher Education, not only to accept the burden that Johnson and Johnson accepts, but, as libraries have throughout the centuries been the keepers of the intellectual light, remain in the forefront of the movement toward equity and intellectual freedom. Libraries need to assume a greater burden–to develop an attitude of "constructive engagement" in addressing the issue of ethnic diversity in the profession.

Briefly, my thesis for today is this:

1. We all must recognize that we have a problem, and that problem is racial. We must all be committed to the search for viable solutions to that problem, both in the long and in the short term.
2. Our solutions–when they come, must be consistent with the overall goals of the library profession.

3. We must work within the bureaucracy for short term solutions; and
4. We must work to change the bureaucracy for long term solutions.

PROBLEMS, PROBLEMS

However it has happened, most of us have become aware that there is a critical shortage of minority librarians. Perhaps you have read the statistics published in the professional literature. Or perhaps you have suddenly observed that your library is plain vanilla, in a rainbow world. Whatever the precipitating event, we have recognized the shortage, and now are moved to do something about it. But what? Where do we start? How do we find the people among what are essentially foreign ethnic groups, and convince them to join us in this profession? What attractions are there to be offered? And what is the reason for the present under representation?

We are all familiar with the multitude of problems which can frustrate our efforts to recruit and retain minority professional staff. The systematic bureaucracy of Civil Service can arrest the most sincere intentions to address past cultural inequities in hiring and promotion. If your staff NEVER quit or retire, and they're not bad enough to fire, you can be stuck with an unhappy situation for a very, very long time. If, however, you believe that this means that you can never change things so why continue to try, then you will never change your present situation.

Yes, these things can take time. It also means that you have to be creative in your thinking, and must be constantly on the lookout for chances to dynamically restructure a staff or department.

Many people will recommend doing a complete analysis of your community to find out what populations are present, served and not served. I feel that if you ask your staff, they will be able to best guess your minority population to within a few percentage points. If you believe that you or some members of your staff are truly in touch with the community, don't be afraid to ask their opinion.

This is not to suggest that doing a complete survey isn't in order. Many times there are small but significant populations present, which you would not dream exist in your community. This past year, I discovered, through our English as a Second Language Literacy Program, that there is a significant French speaking African population in my community. These families and individuals have never been users of our services, although a large number live in a building diagonally across from the library.

In order to serve our community our staff should reflect the ethnic and cultural factors present, to the greatest degree possible. If you read on this subject in the professional literature you will find that there is very little dissent on the existence of the recruitment problem. The problem is methodology, target and resources.

The first place we usually look to recruit a non-professional into school is where we already are–inside the library. Are there likely candidates for librarianship among the non- and para-professionals? Probably, if we can but separate the individual from their current job. Just because a person is checking out books or cards is no reason to believe that person is neither capable of nor interested in working with the public, answering reference questions, coordinating children's services or cataloging the collections. Many of these people have cut short their pursuit of higher education because of the shortage of funds or family responsibilities.

Not only staff, but volunteers, friends of the library, and members of the general population may appear as viable candidates for recruitment. Lets look briefly at some of the factors which influence recruitment, particularly of minorities, into the library profession. The library profession comes to the recruitment effort with several built-in handicaps. Chief among them is the low pay for the amount of education necessary to be a professional. How many other professions require a masters degree, and then have an entry level below 30,000 dollars? Not a lot, especially outside of those other pink collar ghetto professions of teachers and nurses. Even in these other areas, more success has been achieved through powerful concerted action of UNIONS and other organizations, and through critical shortages of trained personnel than has been achieved in librarianship. This pay problem applies to all ethnic groups of course, however the low salaries along with other factors combine to reduce the number of minority recruits attracted to the field.

Librarianship is a profession lacking in prestige in many of the ethnic communities. The recognized disinclination toward reading, recreational or otherwise, by certain of these groups lowers the status of those who choose to pursue careers where reading and understanding written information is essential. In some communities libraries are seen as luxuries, taking time from work or from the family which is not available. "Putting on Airs" is an accusation frequently aimed at those who choose abstract fields of pursuit, such as librarianship, which produce no concrete product and which are not life saving or essential to education. Class and cultural biases can also work against the recruitment of librarians from certain professions. If librarians have traditionally come from the intelligentsia, and ones family is worker/proletarian, one is disinclined to even consider this profession. Conversely, if ones culture has decreed that librarians are traditionally low paid civil servants, and one either is from or aspires to the upper class, this is again a profession that does not merit consideration. Even among mainstream America, there is a neither fish nor fowl feeling about this profession—on the one hand honoring its intellectual requirements while on the other not recognizing and offering the salaries necessary to justify the efforts involved in the education.

Most people, if not all, will concede the need for teachers to be educated, so that they can teach children and thus prepare them for the job market. If you get sick you certainly want a trained and educated nurse and doctor to see to your care. But what does a librarian do? Finds information which someone else produces (the authors) and which many people feel they can live life without.

The discomfort felt by persons of color in coming into the library is further exacerbated by the lack of fellows among the staff. The time when there are "friendly" faces they are likely to be among the non-professionals, maintenance or security staffs, while the professionals, the people at the reference desk are likely to be Caucasian. The scarcity of minority role models then becomes part of the self fulfilling prophesy; if there aren't minority librarians to work with or look up to what is the attraction for someone considering a profession? Who wants to be alone in a group which has in past experience been un-welcoming to hostile? Who will be there to mentor and advise the minority librarian as he/she trains for this new career?

What do you feel like when you walk into a strange neighborhood, and there are no white faces around? In all likelihood you would beat a hasty retreat to an area that was at least mixed races, where you could feel comfortable. Well, that is a BIGGIE for minorities; lack of comfort and assurances of respect can discourage someone from entering a field which, as I have already said, lacks decent pay and the respect of portions of the minority community.

Many of the minorities recruited into the profession will come to the educational process with unusual financial and time responsibilities. Some will be the financial support of not only their individual or nuclear families, but of an extended family. Parents, siblings, and other relations can necessitate extensive financial commitment. Single parenthood is frequently a barrier to continuing education, both emotionally and financially. The scholarship process can alleviate many of the financial difficulties, however the scheduling factors may be insurmountable.

What single parent can leave their child for extended periods to attend school? Even if child care is available, what hours are free from work to do this? With the breakdown of the extended families of previous generations, many African American students are hard pressed to maintain the academic loads necessary to complete a degree while fulfilling the responsibilities of family life. In the Hispanic community also, the increase in the number of families in which all adults work means that there are fewer parents or neighbors staying home and available for the children of the potential student.

As an employer, one must be willing to make special provisions for the employee who is returning to school. If you encourage flexible scheduling, the student will be better able to maintain a significant academic load while also keeping up with the work load. Perhaps arrangements must be made for this student to take off hours during the week, and either use personal or vacation days for this or in part make up the time by working most or all weekends (especially significant if weekend time is premium, i.e., time and a half, etc.).

Even when a member of a minority is interested in librarianship, frequently there has been inadequate preparation for graduate education. Without mentors in elementary and secondary school, priority has seldom been placed on the development of the kind of academic record which lends itself toward a graduate degree.

While some are able to get into college, they are not able to do well enough on the standardized tests to go after a Masters degree. The *Eyes on the Prize* quest for an undergraduate degree may eliminate any possibility of developing the well rounded academic personality which is essential for graduate education. Many students follow the dictum of "If the course is hard and you don't need it to graduate don't take it; finish your education and get to work, and stop wracking up those college loans." In fact family pressure to stop learning and start earning can force a student to do well in an undergraduate major and finish a degree without any idea if he or she will like the job for which they are thereby prepared.

We all have faced the fear of changing jobs. For many in the minority communities the fear of a career change, especially one which necessitates so much preparation and education, is especially daunting. What if this is the wrong choice? Most cannot afford to change again. With the low pay, can they afford to work and go to school for yet another degree to prepare for another job? And what if they cannot succeed in library school? Many have made it through college with family and individual sacrifices, financial and emotional. Having completed that test, often with great difficulty, what is the incentive to take on another challenge, one which promises to be difficult and without great rewards at the end. Thus, having completed college, there is little to encourage a career change, and fear of failure in graduate school combine to further reduce the pool of interested recruits for library education.

Now lets turn several of my previous comments around. I previously said that this profession lacks prestige in some ethnic communities. This is only true among a small number of people in those communities, and reflects past prejudices and beliefs. These are the same cultures which devalue most woman's work if it is outside the home, and which perpetuate the stereotypes of the underclass woman and woman's profession.

Among the larger community, especially the African American community, there is respect for the educated person, and librarianship is accorded similar prestige to other education professionals.

The library represents an underutilized but significant platform from which the black library professional can address community based problems and issues. Librarians of color, with the resources of the library behind them, can more effectively disseminate vital information to the greater community–on issues of culture, health, language enrichment, music, and social issues–than the schools or other public institutions can hope to provide.

The very bureaucracy which I have vilified before guarantees the minority librarian, once hired, a secure path from which to develop a career. Since the Federal Government desegregated the armed forces during World War II, the bureaucracy of Federal and State service has broken ground in bringing down barriers to racial equality. Until recent moves by the private sector to truly recruit qualified minority candidates, and not tokens, this service was a primary method of advancement for minorities, to develop meaningful careers and from which other pursuits such as politics and religious leadership could evolve.

So What Do We Do Now? Let's Be Bold–Lets Be Creative!

Lets look at your staff, as it is today and near term changes. Are there retirements coming up? Has anyone been hinting that they are leaving (You should be so lucky)? What restructuring of the staff would be possible if a professional left?

Think BIG. Don't think about hiring another reference librarian. Especially if you are looking to hire within Civil Service; make the system work for you rather than against you. You know many names are on your certification list. If you know or suspect that there are no minorities, don't use that title. When have you asked for a list for Community Services Librarian? Never? That's the title to use. Outreach Services? Ethnologist? How about library intern, for that person you are bringing along through library school? Run that by sometime; it may get you the person you are looking for.

In or outside Civil Service, be prepared to write a job description which not only meets all the non-discrimination statutes, but will ultimately recruit the person you are looking for. It isn't easy by any means, but it can be done–if you believe in the issue it must be done.

What Strategies Can Be Tried to Retain New Recruits?

Money usually works. If the pay is adequate to the needs of the individual and his/her family, he/she will be less likely to seek a change. If direct salary payments cannot be made more attractive, other job enhancements may be available.

If the staff person is a single parent, finding, arranging for, or subsidizing child care may make remaining on the job not only attractive but possible. If it does not interfere with the performance of the staff person, allowing that recruit to bring his/her child to work occasionally may be the necessary incentive for that person to remain in the job. A professional storyteller in my library brought her daughter to work with her this summer for two days a week, from nine to twelve; this in no way interfered with the functioning of the children's department, and she was able to continue throughout the summer to provide the quality programming which I had come to expect over the course of the last year.

Employers may also find that making sick-child arrangements for their staff will enhance the retention rate; as a mother of two young children, one of my greatest fears is that telephone call in mid-morning, telling me that one of my kids has a fever and needs to be picked up. I have located a local medical center which offers basic sick child care and day care at a reasonable rate; assistance in finding this type of service can earn the undying gratitude of all members of one's staff.

Creative thinking and planning ahead can help an enterprising administrator in the recruitment and retention of minority candidates.

Imagine the vistas which open up with a Principal Library Assistant and a Principal Librarian both leaving at the same time from the same children's department. A Senior Library Assistant and an adult, part time page will remain, as well as the part time storyteller. The total salary budget for the department was $91,429 for the five positions.

With the two departures, a minority intern, already on staff in another department in the Senior Library assistant title ($19,612) is transferred into the children's department, at a salary of $22,000, to be replaced by an entry level Library assistant at $14,963. A professional children's librarian is hired at the recommended salary of $28,500. The adult page become a part time library assistant at a salary of $8,086. The part time storyteller is given two additional steps, from $9,235 to $9,810. The full time library assistant is given an additional step, from $20,830 to $21,320. The total for this new package is $90,513, a saving of $916 and this does not include the saving in the circulation department of $4,649.

The Benefit to the Staff?

1. The addition of an African American professional.
2. The addition of a Spanish speaking professional.
3. The promotion, and therefore the probable continued retention, of an African American storyteller.
4. A salary increment to a valued, experienced para-professional, who was not about to leave but had not in the past had her contributions to the working of the department recognized.
5. A saving to the library of $5,565.

Senior Librarian	$31,219	New Children's Librarian	$28,500
Principal Lib. Asst.	$24,893	Library Intern	$22,678
Senior Lib. Asst.	$20,830	2 step increase	$21,439
PT Storyteller	$9,235	2 step increase	$9,810
PT Adult page	$5,252	PT Lib. Asst.	$8,068
Old Total	$91,429	New Total	$90,513

SAVINGS WITHIN THE DEPARTMENT $916

I am reminded of an incident in a for profit corporation which reflects part of the problem with change. About ten years ago, a major insurance company met to discuss the recruitment of minorities into the sales force. This company was active in the equal rights attempt, and many senior officers had been active in the civil rights movement in the sixties. Almost without exception, these men were sincerely enthusiastic in the effort to recruit more minorities, and especially Hispanics and African Americans, into the work-force.

Needless to say, six months into the process, few minorities had been recruited outside of the home office sphere. When asked about this, each and every Senior Vice President stated that "I'll hire any qualified candidate, black, white, Hispanic, man or woman, who walks through my doors."

In this case there was no secret educational qualification; many of the present salesmen had degrees, but not all. All you had to be was a salesperson, and not particularly a tough one at that. What was happening was the old syndrome; BUSINESS AS USUAL. While these men stated, and may have somehow actually believed, that they were seeking minority candidates, what was actually happening was business as usual. The Vice President for Texas went to his old Alma Mater when he needed recruits. What did he get? Alums from home, and primarily from his old fraternity. In the Massachusetts case, one minority had made it into the recruitment stream; all other recruits were virtual clones of that office's manager.

BUSINESS AS USUAL–If it is allowed to continue, saying that we want change will, in twenty years, find us right where we are today. In order to accomplish real change, fundamental change, the attitudes of recruiters as well as the bureaucracy governing the recruiting must also change.

One of the constant cries which I am certain all administrators have heard is "But we never tried that!" My response is–Well, we're going to try now. If we as library administrators try and fail, *WE* must be willing to assume the responsibility for the failure; if the experiment succeeds, all credit for the success must be shared. But what is failure? As long as one is doing the right things, failures, too, are learning experiences. Let's Learn.

Supplemental Bibliography

Affirmative Action Policies and Practices in ARL Libraries. Compiled by Joyce C. Wright and Barton M. Clark. SPEC Kit 163. Washington, D.C.: Association of Research Libraries, Office of Management Services, 1990.

Armour-Thomas, Eleanor. "Intellectual Assessment of Children from Culturally Diverse Backgrounds," *School Psychology Review,* 29 (1991), p. 273-280.

_____. "Toward an Understanding of Higher Order Thinking Among Minority Students," *Psychology in the Schools,* 29 (1992) p. 273-280.

Belay, Getinet. "Conceptual Strategies for Operationalizing Multi-cultural Curricula," *Journal of Education for Library and Information Science,* 33 (Fall, 1992), p. 295-306.

Brown, Ina. "The Black Information Specialist in the R&D Environment." In *The Black Librarian in America Revisited.* Edited by E.J. Josey. Metuchen, N.J.: Scarecrow Press, 1994. p. 195-206.

Chatman, Elfrieda. "Alienation Theory: Application of a Conceptual Framework to a Study of Information Among Janitors." *RQ,* 29 (Spring, 1990), p. 355-367.

_____. "Diffusion Theory: A Review and Test of a Conceptual Model in Information Diffusion," *Journal of the American Society for Information Science,* 37 (November, 1986), p. 377-386.

_____. "Information, Mass Media Use and the Working Poor," *Library and Information Science Research,* 7 (April, 1985), p. 97-113.

_____. "The Information World of Low Skilled Workers," *Library and Information Science Research,* 9 (October, 1987), p. 265-283.

Collantes, Lourdes. "Agreement in Naming Objects and Concepts in Information Retrieval." Unpublished Ph.D. dissertation, Rutgers University, 1992.

Cultural Diversity Programming in ARL Libraries. Edited by Marilyn Shaver. SPEC Kit 165. Washington, D.C.: Association of Research Libraries, Office of Management Services, 1991.

Figueredo, Danilo. "Developing a Multicultural Collection," *New Jersey Libraries,* 25 (Winter, 1992), p. 13-16.

Franklin, Hardy. "Customer Service: The Heart of the Library," *American Libraries,* 24 (July, 1993), p. 677.

_____. "Customer Service," *School Library Journal,* 39 (August, 1993), p. 4.

Gollop, Claudia. "Selection and Acquisition of Multicultural Materials in the Libraries of the City University of New York," *Urban Academic Librarian,* 8 (Winter, 1991-1992), p. 20-29.

Hacker, Andrew. *Two Nations: Black & White, Separate, Hostile Unequal.* New York: Macmillan, 1992.

Jennings, Kriza A. "Recruiting New Populations to the Library Profession," *Journal of Library Administration*, 14, 3/4 (1993), p. 175-191.

Li, Margaret and Li, Peter, compilers and editors. *Understanding Asian Americans: A Curriculum Resource Guide.* New York: Neal-Schuman, 1990.

Lutzker, Marilyn. *Multiculturalism in the College Curriculum: A Handbook of Strategies and Resources for Faculty.* Westport, CT: Greenwood Press, 1995.

Minority Recruitment and Retention in ARL Libraries. SPEC Kit 167. Washington, D.C.: Association of Research Libraries, Office of Management Services, 1990.

Smith, Karen Patricia, ed. "Multicultural Children's Literature in the United States," *Library Trends,* 41 (Winter, 1993), p. 335-540.

Sullivan, Maureen. "Human Resources in Libraries in the 1990s." In *Library and Information Services Today.* Edited by June Lester. Chicago: American Library Association, 1991. p. 28-41.

Tjoumas, Renee. "Native American Literature for Young People: A Survey of Collection Development Methods in Public Libraries," *Library Trends,* 41 (Winter, 1993), p. 493-523.

Haworth
DOCUMENT DELIVERY
SERVICE

This valuable service provides a single-article order form for any article from a Haworth journal.

- *Time Saving:* No running around from library to library to find a specific article.
- *Cost Effective:* All costs are kept down to a minimum.
- *Fast Delivery:* Choose from several options, including same-day FAX.
- *No Copyright Hassles:* You will be supplied by the original publisher.
- *Easy Payment:* Choose from several easy payment methods.

Open Accounts Welcome for ...
- Library Interlibrary Loan Departments
- Library Network/Consortia Wishing to Provide Single-Article Services
- Indexing/Abstracting Services with Single Article Provision Services
- Document Provision Brokers and Freelance Information Service Providers

---

MAIL or *FAX* THIS ENTIRE ORDER FORM TO:

Haworth Document Delivery Service
The Haworth Press, Inc.
10 Alice Street
Binghamton, NY 13904-1580

or FAX: 1-800-895-0582
or CALL: 1-800-342-9678
9am-5pm EST

PLEASE SEND ME PHOTOCOPIES OF THE FOLLOWING SINGLE ARTICLES:
1) Journal Title: _____

    Vol/Issue/Year:_____Starting & Ending Pages:_____

Article Title:_____

_____

2) Journal Title: _____

    Vol/Issue/Year:_____Starting & Ending Pages:_____

Article Title:_____

_____

3) Journal Title: _____

    Vol/Issue/Year:_____Starting & Ending Pages:_____

Article Title:_____

_____

4) Journal Title: _____

    Vol/Issue/Year:_____Starting & Ending Pages:_____

Article Title:_____

_____

(See other side for Costs and Payment Information)

COSTS: Please figure your cost to order quality copies of an article.

1. Set-up charge per article: $8.00
   ($8.00 × number of separate articles) _____

2. Photocopying charge for each article:

   1-10 pages: $1.00 _____

   11-19 pages: $3.00 _____

   20-29 pages: $5.00 _____

   30+ pages: $2.00/10 pages _____

3. Flexicover (optional): $2.00/article _____

4. Postage & Handling: US: $1.00 for the first article/
   $.50 each additional article _____

   Federal Express: $25.00 _____

   Outside US: $2.00 for first article/
   $.50 each additional article _____

5. Same-day FAX service: $.35 per page _____

   GRAND TOTAL: _____

METHOD OF PAYMENT: (please check one)

❑ Check enclosed ❑ Please ship and bill. PO # _____
(sorry we can ship and bill to bookstores only! All others must pre-pay)

❑ Charge to my credit card: ❑ Visa; ❑ MasterCard; ❑ Discover;
❑ American Express;

Account Number: _____ Expiration date: _____

Signature: ✗ _____

Name: _____ Institution: _____

Address: _____

City: _____ State: _____ Zip: _____

Phone Number: _____ FAX Number: _____

MAIL or *FAX* THIS ENTIRE ORDER FORM TO:

Haworth Document Delivery Service | **or FAX:** 1-800-895-0582
The Haworth Press, Inc. | **or CALL:** 1-800-342-9678
10 Alice Street | 9am-5pm EST)
Binghamton, NY 13904-1580 |